PAGE STREET
PUBLISHING CO.

First published in 2016 by
Page Street Publishing Co.
27 Congress Street, Suite 103
Salem, MA 01970
www.pagestreetpublishing.com

Distributed by Macmillan, sales in Canada by The Canadian Manda Group.

19 18 17 16   1 2 3 4 5

ISBN-13: 978-1-62414-229-1
ISBN-10: 1-62414-229-X

Library of Congress Control Number: 2015952107

Cover and book design by Page Street Publishing Co.
Photography by Jennifer Blume

Printed and bound in China

Page Street is proud to be a member of 1% for the Planet. Members donate one percent of their
sales to one or more of the over 1,500 environmental and sustainability charities across the globe
who participate in this program.

This cookbook is dedicated to all of my clients across the United States, who I call "the warrior mamas." You believed me when I told you to get back into your kitchens. You are doing the hard work, and fighting the good fight. You have loaded your family up with real bone broth and you have healed them. Food is your medicine, food is your poison. Choose your food wisely.

CONTENTS

INTRODUCTION

Bone broth is "the new 1,000-year-old trend." Bone broth has been used by cultures all over the world for centuries to nourish, heal and support the body. Americans who grew up in the 1940s and 1950s reminisce about walking into their mother's kitchen and smelling the aroma of broth cooking on the stove. The broth was touted as a healing elixir and was used as a base for cooking. Jewish grandmothers referred to it as Jewish penicillin.

However, in the 1960s when the trend toward modern food, TV dinners and convenient packaged foods became vogue, Americans moved away from making broth the time-honored way. Instead, they started to reach for pantry, canned or boxed broth. These boxed broths were typically denatured and loaded with flavorings, salts and additives, removing the curative properties of broth altogether.

Today, as more and more Americans are making a shift to using food as medicine, bone broth is now trending back onto our stovetops and into our meals because of the benefits people receive while using the broth as part of their wellness programs. It's rich in nutrients, minerals, amino acids and protein. Drinking broth from a coffee cup is how many people enjoy their broth, while others use it for a base for cooking. *Healing Bone Broth Recipes* gives you recipes that allow you to incorporate the nourishing broth into every meal you make. From waffles to polenta, your meal program will be loaded with the vital nutrients and deep flavors that the broth brings to every dish.

NUTRITION GUIDELINES

OILS AND FATS

Throughout the cookbook we will mention *oil* in recipes. The oils that we approve of as healthy to cook with include all organic coconut oils, ghee, lard, butter, animal fat, avocado oil, olive oil and sesame oil. We never condone the use of canola oil, vegetable oil, corn oil, margarine or any type of fake butter, cooking spray or any other denatured oil. For those of you who have a hard time digesting fat, this is often a gallbladder issue and you most likely need some gallbladder support. Find a practitioner who can suggest a supplement to support your gallbladder for a period of time while your body learns to digest real fats.

SALT

When referring to salt, we use Selina Naturally Celtic sea salt brand. Never use table salt because it's denatured, highly processed and bad for you. Remove it from your pantry and food program indefinitely. Use plenty of Celtic sea salt daily under your practitioner's direction. Celtic sea salt has 80 naturally occurring minerals that are necessary for good health.

MEAT

We source all of our meat from organic, pasture-raised animals. Beef should always be grass-fed, grass-finished organic beef. Please keep in mind that cows can be called grass-fed and then finished the last remaining months of their lives fed with grain. Always choose grass-fed, grass-finished beef. Chicken should be organic and pasture-raised. Never choose farmed fish; instead always purchase wild caught.

VEGETABLES

Organic vegetables are free of pesticides that cause cancer. Please always source organic vegetables and support the farmers who care about your health and our environment.

RICE

I don't eat rice because it doesn't sit well with me. Many of you have requested recipes with rice. We have provided some recipes with rice but know that rice isn't true Paleo. Many of the rice recipes can be substituted using cauliflower rice for the strict Paleoites. For those of you who follow a modified version of a Paleo diet, please always presoak your rice, grains and oatmeal. It is simple to do, and it will break down the phytic acid in the rice, which can wreak havoc on your digestive system. The soaking method for rice is 1 cup (190 g) rice to 2 cups (480 ml) liquid. For example, take 1 cup (190 g) of rice and add 2 cups (480 ml) of warm water with ½ teaspoon of apple cider vinegar and cover overnight in a cupboard. The next day simply strain the rice and add 1 cup (240 ml) of liquid and cook. For our recipes, the liquid you add will be bone broth, of course.

PASTA

We do not cook with pasta as pasta is an empty food, void of nutrition. Instead, we use zoodles (noodles made from zucchini), kelp noodles, Paleo noodles or spaghetti squash. If you must use pasta, you should use a quinoa or rice pasta.

DAIRY

Many strict Paleoites will not consume dairy; however there is a very large majority of people who follow a Paleo program and allow raw dairy. Raw dairy is in its most natural state and is never heated. If you are going to consume dairy, it should always be raw, never pasteurized. Look for raw milk and raw cheese at your natural grocers.

NUT MILKS

We do not support the use of commercially prepared nut milks such as almond milk, cashew milk or coconut milk. We do, however, love real organic coconut milk from a BPA-free can without anything added. If you look at the nut milks that are in the refrigerated sections in stores, you will find them loaded with chemicals and additives that make these milks toxic to the body. Again, homemade milk is perfectly fine, and plain organic coconut milk is very healthy for you. Also, there are new companies that are making "homemade" nut milks. Check the ingredients.

SUGAR

The only sweeteners you should consume are raw honey, grade B maple syrup, coconut sugar or stevia in its most natural state. These sweeteners should not be used daily in coffee, tea or treats. You should consume them sparingly. If you have a sugar addiction, stop consuming sugar for 6 weeks, do the 6-week clearing program and you will kick your sugar craving.

WATER

Drink plenty of clean water (filtered) every day. Want to know how much? Take your weight, divide it in half and drink that amount in ounces. For example, if you weigh 150 pounds and divide that in half, you have 75. So drink 75 ounces (2.1 L) of water per day. If you use a reverse osmosis water filtration system, always add minerals back to the system or consume them via a high-quality supplement to avoid becoming mineral deficient.

GRAINS

Obviously Paleoites do not consume grains and do not recognize grains as part of a wellness plan. If you follow the Weston A. Price camp, you know that soaking your grains or consuming sprouted grains is the ideal way to eat grains, and that grains are encouraged in your meal plan. Whatever plan you choose, take an individual approach. I cannot eat grains. I can soak them, sprout them, grow them, massage them and even try to have a non-denatured grain such as einkorn wheat, and I still cannot tolerate grains. Even after doing the gut and psychology syndrome (GAPS) program, I could not add in a grain, which leads me to my theory that you must take an individual approach to your food program. I tend to take a Paleo approach to my food plan because it suits me well. I suggest you do my 6-week clearing program; after 6 weeks of clearing you can introduce properly prepared grains if you really desire to do so. If you can tolerate them, add them into your diet, but recognize that the main source of your nourishment will come from the meat, vegetables and small amounts of fruit you consume. If you feel sluggish, bloated, experience joint pain, fogginess or a myriad of other symptoms, you may be someone who does not tolerate grains.

BONE BROTH BASICS

CHICKEN BONE BROTH

This Chicken Bone Broth recipe is the broth that you will be using for every recipe in this book that calls for "Chicken Bone Broth." I suggest making a batch and then storing it in freezer-safe mason jars. If you don't have time to make your own chicken bone broth, you can purchase my Real Bone Broth online or find it in the freezer section at a natural grocer near you.

SERVES 3 TO 4

2 to 3 lb (908–1,362 g) bones such as necks, backs, breastbones and wings

2 to 4 chicken feet (this makes the broth extra gelatinous but it is optional)

16 cups (4 L) cold filtered water

2 tbsp (30 ml) organic apple cider vinegar

1 large onion, chopped

2 cloves garlic, whole

Sea salt to taste, we recommend Selina Naturally Celtic

1 bunch organic fresh parsley

Place all the ingredients except for the parsley in a large stockpot and bring to a boil. Skim and discard the top layer after boiling and then slow simmer for 24 hours. Add water if necessary, but if you low simmer you may not need to. During the last hour of cooking, add fresh parsley to pull additional minerals from the bones. Strain the broth and serve or freeze for later use.

BEEF BONE BROTH

Real Beef Bone Broth is, shall we say, "meaty." My clients love the heartiness of this broth and true meat lovers will adore the flavor that comes from the bones. As with my Chicken Bone Broth recipe, I suggest making this recipe ahead of time and storing it in freezer-safe mason jars. If you don't have time to make your own broth for the recipes in this cookbook, you can always order my Real Bone Broth online or find it in the freezer section of your natural grocer.

SERVES 3 TO 4

4 lb (1.8 kg) knuckle bones, mixed bones and marrow

1 calves foot, cut into pieces (optional)

3 lb (1.3 kg) rib or neck bones

16 cups (4 L) or more cold filtered water

½ cup (120 ml) organic apple cider vinegar

3 onions, coarsely chopped

3 cloves of whole fresh garlic

Several sprigs of fresh thyme, tied together (for flavor, optional)

1 tsp dried green peppercorns, crushed (optional)

Sea salt to taste, we recommend Selina Naturally Celtic

1 bunch parsley

Preheat the oven to 350°F (180°C). Place all bones on a roasting pan and brown in the oven. When well browned, add to a large stockpot along with all the juices from pan. Add all the other ingredients. Add additional water, if necessary, to cover the bones. Bring to a boil, remove first layer after an hour, then return to a low simmer for 48 hours, adding additional water if needed. Strain broth and serve or freeze for later use.

HEALING BREAKFASTS

When your mom told you that breakfast was the most important meal of the day, she was right! The word *breakfast* actually means to break your fast. After your body has been fasting through the night, it needs nourishment from the foods you eat when you wake up to be able to function and perform optimally. Ensuring your body receives the proper amounts of fat, protein and carbohydrates in the morning will not only help to fuel you for your day, but will also boost your resting metabolism.

This chapter includes some of my favorite easy breakfast ideas that will keep you energized throughout your day.

SAVORY BONE BROTH WAFFLES

The name of this dish speaks for itself. We came up with this dish out of the need to hide broth in everything we cooked, even some of the sweet things we love like waffles. The broth smooths out the coconut flour, and you will be hard-pressed to tell the difference between these waffles and waffles made with flour. The savory waffle is perfect with maple syrup and crumbled crispy bacon. Our social media followers love the concept of this recipe, and the waffles taste amazing!

SERVES 4 TO 6

1 cup (115 g) coconut flour

¾ cup (100 g) arrowroot or tapioca flour

2 tsp (10 g) baking powder

½ tsp sea salt, we recommend Selina Naturally Celtic

2 large organic eggs, separated

½ cup (120 ml) melted coconut oil

1½ cups (360 ml) Chicken Bone Broth (page 10)

1 tbsp (15 ml) honey

Ghee or oil, for coating waffle iron

4 slices of cooked crispy bacon, chopped

1 pat of butter, and maple syrup, for garnish

Preheat the waffle iron. Put the coconut flour, arrowroot or tapioca flour, baking powder and salt in a mixing bowl and combine well. Add the egg yolks, oil, bone broth and honey, whisking together to combine ingredients completely. In a separate bowl, whisk the egg whites until fluffy and fold into batter. Coat the waffle iron with ghee or oil and pour batter into the waffle iron and cook until golden and slightly crispy. Serve topped with crispy cooked bacon, a pat of butter, maple syrup or your choice of toppings.

SAVORY OATMEAL FOR BREAKFAST

This Paleo oatmeal can be made with either oats, for those of you who include them in your food program, or by preparing fake oatmeal using coconut flour. I use coconut flour "oatmeal" and then eat a big side of bacon with this dish. Oatmeal is not the most nutritious breakfast, but we get a lot of requests for something other than eggs, and you can certainly add this to break up your breakfast choices one day per week. I tell all of my clients to do the 90-10 rule. Eat perfectly for 90 percent of the time; for the other 10 percent, allow yourself to cheat. When you do eat carbohydrate-ladened breakfasts, it is a good idea to eat plenty of fat with the meal such as ghee, butter or coconut oil. The fat will slow the rate at which your blood sugar spikes. It will help prevent the extreme highs and lows when loading up on carbs. This is a good idea when you eat potatoes, sweet potatoes and yams as well. If you choose to use oats in this recipe, you will always want to soak the grains the night before (see the Nutrition Guidelines section on page 7) for directions.

SERVES 4 TO 6

1 cup (80 g) organic oatmeal

1 cup (240 ml) warm water

1 tbsp (15 ml) apple cider vinegar

1 cup (240 ml) Chicken Bone Broth (page 10)

Sea salt to taste, we recommend Selina Naturally Celtic

¼ cup (45 g) grated Parmesan cheese

2 slices crumbled bacon

1 tsp fresh chives

Soak the oatmeal, water and vinegar in a small pot overnight (this breaks down the phytic acid in the oats and makes it easier to digest). In the morning, mix in the bone broth and salt and cook for 5 to 10 minutes on low; be careful not to burn it. Remove from heat and add in Parmesan cheese, crumbled bacon and chives, stirring well.

BACON AND TOMATO BREAKFAST CASSEROLE

Everything is better with bacon, wouldn't you agree? I like to make the bacon extra crispy for this recipe
to add that extra crunch when you bite into a serving. The bone broth blends all the flavors together
for a smooth, fluffy casserole that is perfect for weekday breakfasts or weekend company.
This one is sure to impress your guests.

SERVES 4 TO 6

¼ cup (60 ml) extra-virgin olive oil, plus
more for baking dish and foil

1 lb (450 g) gluten-free, grain-free
baguette cut into 1-inch (2.5-cm) cubes

1 lb (450 g) sliced organic bacon, cut
into ½-inch (1.3-cm) pieces

⅓ cup onion, chopped

1 (28-oz [790-ml]) can whole organic
Italian tomatoes, drained, chopped and
patted dry

½ tsp crushed red pepper flakes

2 cups (230 g) extra-sharp raw cheddar
cheese, shredded

2 cups (230 g) raw Monterey Jack
cheese, shredded

2 tbsp (25 g) chives, chopped

1¾ cups (415 ml) Chicken Bone Broth
(page 10)

Sea salt to taste, we recommend Selina
Naturally Celtic

8 large organic eggs

Preheat the oven to 350°F (180°C). Lightly oil a 9×13-inch (23×33-cm) glass
baking dish. In a large bowl, toss the bread with the olive oil and spread on a large-
rimmed baking sheet. Bake for about 20 minutes, tossing until the bread is golden
and lightly crisp.

In a large skillet, cook the bacon over moderately high heat until crisp. Transfer
the bacon to paper towels to drain; reserve 2 tablespoons (30 ml) of the fat in
the skillet.

Add the onion to the skillet and cook over moderate heat, stirring occasionally
until softened, about 5 minutes. Add the tomatoes and crushed red pepper and
cook until any liquid is evaporated, about 3 minutes.

Return the toasted bread cubes to the bowl. Add the contents of the skillet along
with the bacon, shredded cheeses, chives and broth. Stir until the bread is evenly
moistened. Season with salt. Spread the mixture in the baking dish and cover with
lightly oiled foil. Bake the bread mixture in the oven for 30 minutes. Remove the
foil and bake until the top is crisp, about 15 minutes more. Remove the baking
dish from the oven and use a ladle to press 8 indentations into the bread mixture.
Crack an egg into each indentation. Return the dish to the oven and bake for about
15 minutes until the egg whites are set.

BREAKFAST SAUSAGE, BACON AND POTATO SOUP

This dish is another fantastic way to incorporate soup into your breakfast rotation. It's rich, creamy, loaded with protein and will keep you full and satisfied for hours.

SERVES 4 TO 6

2 lb (1 kg) Yukon gold potatoes, soaked, peeled and quartered

1 pinch sea salt, we recommend Selina Naturally Celtic

2 cups (480 ml) Chicken Bone Broth (page 10)

1 cup (240 ml) raw heavy cream

1 cup (240 ml) whole raw milk

2 tbsp (30 g) unsalted butter

1 garlic clove, minced

¼ tsp nutmeg

Freshly ground pepper, to taste

4 slices of bacon

2 organic breakfast sausage links

1 tsp apple cider vinegar

4 large organic eggs

2 tbsp (10 g) minced chives

In a large saucepan, cover the potatoes with water and bring to a boil. Add a large pinch of salt and boil over moderately high heat until the potatoes are tender, about 25 minutes. Drain well and remove potatoes.

Add the broth, cream and milk to the saucepan and bring to a boil over moderate heat. Stir in the butter, garlic and nutmeg. Add the potato pieces a few at a time and with an immersion blender, purée until very smooth. Season with pepper and keep warm.

In a medium skillet, cook the bacon over moderate heat until crisp. Transfer the bacon to paper towels to drain, then break into pieces. Pour off most of the fat from the skillet. Add the sausages to the skillet and cook over moderate heat until browned, about 5 to 7 minutes. Remove the sausages from the skillet and chop. Fill a medium-deep skillet with water and bring to a boil; reduce the heat to maintain a gentle simmer. Add the vinegar, crack each egg into a ramekin and then slide the egg into the simmering water. Poach over moderately low heat until the whites are just firm and the yolks are runny, about 3 minutes.

Ladle the soup into shallow bowls. Top with the bacon, sausage and well-drained poached eggs. Garnish with the chives.

BREAKFAST STEW

Americans need to have a paradigm shift when it comes to breakfast. Breakfast does not have to be dry cereal, pancakes and waffles. Those breakfast foods will leave your body starved for nutrition and your blood sugar peaking and dropping within a very short time. However, you can also get in a rut of eating eggs every day. I suggest starting your day with soup as one of the steps to better health. Some of the healthiest societies in the world start their days off with some type of soup, pho or broth for breakfast. I often tell my clients to have soup a few days a week for better health. This breakfast stew is a nice bridge from cereal to soup. This is a great first recipe to get the family familiar with what breakfast can look like in your home, and to start making the change from cereal to nourishing foods.

SERVES 4 TO 6

1½ tsp (7 ml) extra-virgin olive oil

1 garlic clove

1 onion, sliced

2 organic chorizo chicken sausages, finely chopped

4 pieces crispy nitrate-free bacon, chopped

1 cup (160 g) organic diced tomatoes

2 tbsp (30 g) tomato paste

½ cup (120 ml) Chicken Bone Broth (page 10)

1 tsp chili powder

½ tsp smoked paprika

Sea salt to taste, we recommend Selina Naturally Celtic

Dash freshly ground pepper

½ tsp crushed red pepper flakes

3 cups (720 ml) water

2 tsp (10 ml) vinegar

3 large organic eggs

Heat the oil and garlic in a medium-sized pot. Add the onion and sauté for 5 minutes. Add in chopped sausage and cook, stirring until the sausage is cooked. Cook the bacon until crispy; drain on paper towels and set aside. Add diced tomatoes, tomato paste, chicken bone broth and spices into the pot and mix. Reduce heat to a simmer.

Heat the water and add in a dash of vinegar. Crack 1 egg into a ramekin. Right before boiling, use a spoon and swirl the water. Drop the egg into the water and allow it to cook for 1 to 2 minutes. Carefully spoon out the poached egg and serve over the stew.

SUN-DRIED TOMATO AND ITALIAN SAUSAGE FRITTATA

Sun-dried tomatoes have an intense sweet-tart flavor. A little goes a long way in a casserole. I love how the Italian sausage complements them in this casserole. This is a great breakfast for company and we like to make it as a grab-and-go breakfast when we are short for time. We make it in advance, cut it into slices, and grab it on our way out the door.

SERVES 6

1 diced shallot

2 garlic cloves, minced

1 cup (175 g) chopped sun-dried tomatoes

2 tbsp (30 ml) olive oil

4 chicken Italian sausages, casing removed

1 tbsp (3 g) dried thyme

½ cup (120 ml) Chicken Bone Broth (page 10)

Salt and pepper

6 large organic eggs, beaten

1 cup (115 g) raw cheddar cheese (optional)

In a large cast-iron skillet, sauté the shallot, garlic and sun-dried tomatoes in olive oil until slightly browned. Add in the chicken sausage, thyme and the chicken bone broth. Cook until the bone broth has been absorbed. Add salt and pepper to taste. In a large bowl beat the eggs, add salt, pepper and cheese (if using) to the eggs. Once the sausage is cooked through, pour the egg mixture into the cast-iron skillet; do not mix. Allow it to cook on the stove until the eggs are still slightly runny on top. Remove the skillet from the stove and place in broiler for 2 to 3 minutes or until the top has slightly browned.

JALAPEÑO SWEET POTATO HASH WITH FRIED EGGS

My sister Trish is an amazing cook. When she comes to visit, my children will give her a list of foods they want her to make. This breakfast dish is one of her signature dishes. The sweet potatoes actually become a little caramelized and they soften with the broth. Then the jalapeño gives it a little kick so it's a sweet and spicy combination in your mouth. I like to place the fried eggs on top and mix together on my plate.

SERVES 4 TO 6

2 tbsp (30 g) butter, ghee or coconut oil

1 shallot, chopped

1 medium yellow onion, sliced

4 sweet potatoes, peeled and diced

½ cup (120 ml) Chicken Bone Broth (page 10)

1 jalapeño, seeds removed and chopped

Sea salt to taste, we recommend Selina Naturally Celtic

Freshly ground pepper, to taste

Garlic powder, to taste

In a large cast-iron skillet, melt the butter over medium heat. Add in the shallot and yellow onion and cook until translucent. Add in the diced sweet potatoes and mix well. Allow to cook for 3 to 5 minutes. Add in the bone broth to deglaze the pan and allow it to cook until the broth has been absorbed. Add in the jalapeño, sea salt, pepper and garlic powder. Stir well and allow to cook until the sweet potatoes are soft, about 10 to 15 minutes.

HOMEMADE MAPLE AND APPLE BREAKFAST SAUSAGES WITH ROSEMARY

Most people don't realize how much sugar they consume in a day. Sugar is hidden in many foods, even ketchup. I always know my sugarholic clients when one of the first questions they ask is what sweeteners they are allowed to use. This is a recipe a client gave me when she replaced her sugar-filled breakfast sausage. I make a few batches of these sausages and freeze them alongside coconut pancakes. Then we wrap them up and take them for on-the-go snacks and light lunches.

SERVES 6 TO 8

½ lb (225 g) organic ground pork

½ lb (225 g) organic ground beef

2 cloves fresh garlic, minced

1 tsp sea salt, we recommend Selina Naturally Celtic

½ tsp dried thyme

1 tsp rosemary

¼ tsp onion powder

¼ tsp dried oregano

¼ tsp dried basil

1 medium sweet organic apple, peeled and finely diced

2 tbsp (30 ml) organic grade B maple syrup

2 tbsp (30 g) ghee, butter or coconut oil

4 tbsp (59 ml) Beef Bone Broth (page 11)

In a large bowl combine pork, beef, garlic, seasonings, apple and maple syrup. Form the mixture into patties. In a large cast-iron skillet, melt your ghee on medium to high heat until the skillet is hot. Cook the patties for 10 to 12 minutes on each side or until browned. While the breakfast sausages are cooking, add 1 tablespoon (15 ml) of broth at a time to keep the patties from drying out.

BROCCOLI AND CAULIFLOWER HAM CASSEROLE

If you have thyroid issues, you have probably been told to stay away from cruciferous vegetables. However, if cooked, they are fine in small amounts. I like to make this casserole and then cut it into squares, wrap them individually and take them with me to the office for breakfast. This is also great for school lunches. I trained my children from an early age to eat real food cold. In other words, it's okay to have a school lunch with cold chicken or a cold casserole. Train your kids early and they will never find the need for a microwave, and you will never fall into the rut of making your kids sandwiches for lunch every day.

SERVES 6 TO 8

---

1 large yellow onion

2 cloves garlic

1 tbsp (15 g) butter

5 cups (1.2 L) Chicken Bone Broth (page 10)

2 lb (900 g) cauliflower, divided

¾ cup (180 ml) milk

½ tsp sea salt, we recommend Selina Naturally Celtic

1 head broccoli

7 oz (200 g) cooked ham, sliced

1 heaping cup (115 g) raw cheddar cheese, shredded

Preheat the oven to 400°F (200°C). Cut the onion into thin slices. Chop the garlic cloves. Melt the butter in a skillet on low heat, add the onion and garlic and sauté on low until the onions are golden and caramelized, about 20 minutes. Set aside. Bring the chicken broth to a boil. Cut half of the cauliflower into cubes using the stalks and stems, setting aside most of the whole florets, and cook the cubes in the broth until tender, 5 to 7 minutes. Reserve ½ cup (120 ml) of the broth, drain the rest.

To make the creamy white sauce, place the tender cauliflower cubes into a blender or food processor together with the caramelized onions, garlic, reserved broth, milk and salt. Purée until smooth.

Divide the remaining 1 pound (450 g) of cauliflower and the broccoli into rosettes. Bring a large pot of salted water to a boil and cook the cauliflower rosettes for 5 minutes. Add the broccoli rosettes and cook for another 3 minutes. Drain, then place the cauliflower and broccoli rosettes in a large casserole dish together with the ham slices. Pour the creamy cauliflower sauce over the top and sprinkle with shredded cheese. Bake for 20 to 30 minutes until the cheese is melted, bubbly and golden.

BRUSSELS SPROUT AND SWEET POTATO HASH WITH GROUND BEEF

This is a great dish for Brussels sprout lovers. My daughter Camden loves Brussels sprouts, but only after I roasted them in the oven with grade B maple syrup. Once I introduced them in that manner, I was able to slip them into these types of recipes below. The sweet potato adds a sweetness that pairs well with the slightly nutty flavor of the Brussels sprouts. My daughter actually asks for Brussels sprouts for dinner when I ask her what side dishes she wants. I love starting the day off with this dish.

SERVES 6

1 tbsp (15 g) ghee or coconut oil

½ cup (40 g) chopped onion

Garlic powder

½ cup (60 g) grated sweet potato

¼ cup (60 ml) Beef Bone Broth (page 11)

1 lb (450 g) grass-fed, ground beef

¾ cup (255 g) shredded Brussels sprouts

Sea salt to taste, we recommend Selina Naturally Celtic

1 large organic egg, cooked any style

In a cast-iron skillet, heat the ghee over a medium flame. Once it's warm, add the onion and garlic powder, and sauté until the onion is soft and translucent. Add the sweet potato and continue to sauté for a few minutes longer. Add in the broth and simmer until the broth is absorbed. Add the beef and cook until the meat has browned and is fully cooked. Add the Brussels sprouts and sauté for about 5 more minutes until they are bright green and a bit crispy. Salt to taste and top with a cooked egg to your choice—we love ours fried with a runny yolk!

GRAIN-FREE BISCUITS AND BONE BROTH GRAVY

After eating these biscuits and gravy you will never go back to Mama's southern cooking.
There is no need. The tapioca flour ensures these biscuits aren't too dense. Using real bone broth
as opposed to canned chicken stock gives this dish delicious depth.

SERVES 6 TO 8

1 cup (125 g) tapioca flour

2 tbsp (15 g) coconut flour

½ tsp sea salt, we recommend Selina Naturally Celtic

1 tsp onion powder

1 tsp garlic powder

10 tbsp (148 ml) unsalted grass-fed butter, melted

2 large organic eggs

¼ cup (60 ml) warm water

1 lb (450 g) Italian sausage

2 tbsp (30 g) ghee or grass-fed butter

2 large yellow onions, roughly chopped

5 garlic cloves, minced

1 tbsp (2 g) minced fresh sage

1 tbsp (2 g) minced fresh thyme

1 tbsp (2 g) minced fresh rosemary

1 tsp dried oregano

4 cups (960 ml) Chicken Bone Broth (page 10)

½ tsp sea salt, we recommend Selina Naturally Celtic, adjust to taste

½ tsp black pepper, to taste

Preheat the oven to 350°F (180°C).

Place flours, salt, onion powder and garlic powder in a large bowl. Mix with your hands or a fork. Combine until the mixture is a yellowish-white color. In a small bowl whisk the melted butter and eggs to combine. Add the egg mixture to the dry ingredients and whisk until a batter is created. Add the water and stir until well combined. Line a muffin tin with parchment liners and scoop 2 tablespoons (30 g) of the mixture into each cup. Transfer to the oven and bake for 30 minutes. Remove from the oven and let cool.

Remove the Italian sausage from its casing, break it apart, cook thoroughly in a cast-iron skillet and set it aside. Melt the ghee in a pot over medium heat and add the onions. Cook for 15 minutes or until the onions begin to turn golden brown. Add the garlic and herbs and sauté for a minute. Add the broth to deglaze the pan and increase the heat to high. Once the mixture comes to a boil, reduce the heat to a simmer. Cover the pot and cook for 20 to 30 minutes or until the mixture reduces by half. Add salt and pepper to taste. Place the remaining sauce into a blender. Purée until smooth. Add the cooked sausage to the pot and return the gravy to the pot, mixing well. Top the biscuits with sausage gravy to serve.

BREAKFAST MUSH

Don't be fooled by the name of this dish—it is really good. This is one of the first dishes that my clients can eat after coming off of chicken soup for their first two days on the 6-week clearing program. We have it listed as breakfast, but you can eat it at any time of the day. Make plenty because you will find yourself eating an entire plate of this.

SERVES 6

---

2 tbsp (30 g) ghee

1 medium yellow onion, diced

2 medium zucchini, diced

1 yellow squash, diced

2 cloves garlic, minced

1 lb (450 g) grass-fed ground beef

Sea salt to taste, we recommend Selina Naturally Celtic

Freshly ground pepper, to taste

½ cup (120 ml) Beef Bone Broth (page 11)

In a medium-sized skillet, heat the ghee over medium heat and sauté the onion, zucchini, squash and garlic until the onion is translucent. Once translucent, add the ground beef, salt and pepper. Break the beef apart with a wooden spoon and cook thoroughly. Once cooked through, add the beef bone broth and scrape the bottom of the pan well. Stir, cover and allow to simmer on low heat until the bone broth is absorbed.

NOURISHING SIDES AND STARTERS

Sometimes the appetizers can be the best part of a meal. The starters can really set the tone for your dinner party or family dinner. In fact, I have been known to order a variety of starters at a restaurant as my meal. The bone broth in these recipes adds the extra flavor often needed in sides and is what really sets them apart.

BRAISED ENDIVE WITH ORANGE

The sweet zest of orange in this dish is refreshing and complements the endives bitterness perfectly. Make sure you hand-squeeze your own orange juice in this recipe; the quality of fresh-squeezed oranges can't compare to sugar-laden, store-bought juice!

SERVES 6

---

3 tbsp (45 ml) extra-virgin olive oil, divided

10 medium Belgian endives, halved lengthwise

½ cup (120 ml) Chicken Bone Broth (page 10), divided

Sea salt, we recommend Selina Naturally Celtic

Freshly ground black pepper

1 cup (240 ml) fresh squeeze, organic orange juice, divided

4 tbsp (60 g) unsalted butter

2 tbsp (30 ml) honey

2 scallions, white and pale green parts only, thinly sliced

2 tbsp (20 g) salted roasted pumpkin seeds

Balsamic vinegar, for drizzling

You will need 2 large skillets for this dish to make enough endive. In each of the 2 large skillets, heat 1½ tablespoons (22 ml) of the extra-virgin olive oil. Add the endive halves cut sides down and cook over medium heat until lightly browned, about 5 minutes. Add ¼ cup (60 ml) broth into each skillet and reduce by about half, about 2 to 3 minutes. Turn the endives over, season with salt and pepper and add ½ cup (120 ml) of the orange juice to each skillet. Cover and cook over low heat. Turn once and cook until tender, about 10 to 15 minutes. Remove the endives and place on serving platter with cut sides up. Combine the liquid in both skillets into one. Add the butter and honey and boil over high heat until it's a syrup consistency, about 4 minutes. Season with salt and pepper. Pour the sauce over the endives and garnish with the sliced scallions and pumpkin seeds. Drizzle the endives with the balsamic vinegar and serve.

BACON AND CHEESE
MASHED SWEET POTATOES

This side dish can replace the old mashed potatoes standby. The savory bacon and the sweet potatoes are the perfect combination. We love to pair these with a delicious grass-fed steak to satisfy that all-American meat-and-potato craving.

SERVES 6 TO 8

1 lb (450 g) nitrate-free smoked bacon

½ cup (120 ml) grade B maple syrup, plus more for drizzling

5 lb (2.2 kg) sweet potatoes, peeled and cubed

Sea salt to taste, we recommend Selina Naturally Celtic

2 cups (480 ml) Chicken Bone Broth (page 10)

1 stick butter cut into pieces

3 cups (362 g) raw cheddar cheese, grated

Coarse black pepper

Nutmeg to taste

Preheat the oven to 400°F (200°C). Arrange the bacon on a wire rack over a baking sheet and bake until crisp, 10 to 15 minutes. Remove from the oven and raise the heat to 450°F (230°C). Brush the bacon with maple syrup and return it to the oven for 2 to 3 minutes to glaze. Let the bacon cool and then chop and set aside. Place the potatoes in a pot, cover with water and bring to a boil. Salt the water and cook until tender, about 20 to 30 minutes, then drain and return them to the pot. Add the broth ½ cup (120 ml) at a time and mash to make the potatoes smooth. Once mashed, stir in the butter and cheese and season with salt, pepper and nutmeg to taste. To serve, top with chopped bacon and drizzle with a ½ tablespoon (7 ml) of maple syrup.

THYME AND BONE BROTH BRAISED BRUSSELS SPROUTS

This simple preparation of Brussels sprouts brings out their natural sweetness when slightly caramelized. We love to pair these with roasted or braised proteins!

SERVES 4 TO 6

1 tbsp (15 ml) extra-virgin olive oil

2 shallots, sliced

1 lb (450 g) Brussels sprouts, trimmed

1 cup (240 ml) Chicken Bone Broth (page 10)

1½ tsp (1 g) chopped fresh thyme or ½ tsp dried

¼ tsp sea salt, we recommend Selina Naturally Celtic

¼ tsp freshly ground pepper

Heat the oil in a large skillet over medium-high heat. Add the shallots and Brussels sprouts and cook, stirring often, until the shallots start to brown and the Brussels sprouts are browned in spots, 2 to 4 minutes. Stir in the broth, thyme, salt and pepper. Cover and reduce the heat to medium-low. Cook until the Brussels sprouts are tender, 10 to 15 minutes.

CREAMY PARSNIPS AND SPINACH

There is something so comforting about good old creamed spinach. Adding parsnips gives this dish
a subtle sweetness that pairs perfectly with the creamy, rich qualities of this dish. Serve this alongside our
Blue Cheese Crusted Filet Mignon (page 133) for a meal that is sure to impress.

SERVES 4 TO 6

4 tbsp (60 g) unsalted butter, divided

2 tbsp (30 g) coconut oil

2 lb (900 g) small parsnips, cut into
¾-inch (2-cm) pieces

2 large shallots, thinly sliced

1 cup (240 ml) Beef Bone Broth
(page 11)

1 tsp chopped thyme

Sea salt, we recommend Selina
Naturally Celtic

Freshly ground pepper

¼ lb (600 g) baby spinach

1 tbsp (15 g) arrowroot powder

2 cups (240 ml) raw milk

½ tsp freshly grated nutmeg

In a large, deep skillet, melt 2 tablespoons (30 g) of the butter in the oil. Add the parsnips and cook over medium-high heat until lightly browned, about 6 minutes. Add the shallots and cook until softened, about 3 minutes. Add the broth and thyme and bring to a boil. Add salt and pepper to taste; cover and simmer over low heat until the parsnips are tender, about 8 minutes.

Meanwhile, fill a large pot with 2 inches (5 cm) of water and bring to a boil. Add the spinach in large handfuls and blanch, stirring just until wilted. Drain and cool under running water. Squeeze the spinach dry and coarsely chop. Stir the spinach into the parsnips. In a medium saucepan, melt the remaining 2 tablespoons (30 g) of butter over moderately high heat until lightly browned. Whisk in the arrowroot and cook, whisking for 1 minute. Whisk in raw milk and nutmeg, season with salt and pepper and bring the sauce to a boil, whisking until thickened. Stir the sauce into the spinach and parsnips and bring to a simmer, continue to cook for 5 minutes. Add more broth if it is too thick. Transfer to a serving bowl and serve.

BLACK RICE WITH GREEN ONIONS AND EGG

The Paleo version of this side dish can simply be made by substituting prepared cauliflower rice in place of the black rice. You can then add the bone broth as you sauté all the ingredients together. Either option will yield a ton of nutrients and flavor. Should you choose to make this dish using the black rice, remember to soak the rice the night before to break down the phytic acid (see page 7 for soaking instructions). You could also sneak this recipe in as a breakfast choice, particularly if you are working out in the morning.

SERVES 4 TO 6

1 cup (145 g) black rice, soaked overnight

2 cups (480 ml) Chicken Bone Broth (page 10)

2 large organic eggs

1 tbsp (15 ml) sesame oil

2 tbsp (30 g) coconut oil

2 cloves garlic, minced

1½ tsp (7 g) minced fresh ginger

Sea salt to taste, we recommend Selina Naturally Celtic

Freshly ground pepper

2 green onions, sliced

Add rice and the chicken bone broth to a saucepan. Bring to a boil over high heat. Once boiling, cover and lower to a simmer. Cook for 15 to 20 minutes until the rice is tender. There should be no liquid left in the pan. Remove from the heat, remove lid, fluff the rice with a fork and set aside. Whisk eggs in a bowl. In a large skillet, heat the oils over high heat. Add the eggs and cook thoroughly, about 2 minutes, chopping into small pieces. Add garlic, ginger, rice, salt and pepper. Continue to cook until some of the rice becomes crispy. Remove from the heat. Season with salt and pepper to taste and serve with a garnish of green onions.

GOAT CHEESE AND SUN-DRIED TOMATO POLENTA BITES

These bites are perfect for entertaining guests. The goat cheese is rich and creamy, while the sun-dried tomato and pesto provide an acidity that balances the flavors perfectly.

SERVES 4 TO 6

⅓ cup (80 ml) extra-virgin olive oil or bacon grease

2²/₃ cups (630 ml) Beef or Chicken Bone Broth (page 11 or 10)

1 sprig fresh rosemary

1 clove garlic, peeled and crushed

1 cup (160 g) polenta

8 oz (310 g) basil pesto

2 oz (60 g) raw milk goat cheese, separated into small chunks

⅓ cup (20 g) sun-dried tomatoes packed in oil, drained and chopped

Sea salt to taste, we recommend Selina Naturally Celtic

Lightly oil a 13 × 9-inch (33 × 23-cm) baking pan. Combine the first three ingredients and place in a saucepan over medium heat and simmer for 5 minutes. Using a slotted spoon, remove the garlic and the herbs. Whisk in the polenta very slowly, then return to a boil. Reduce the heat to low. Simmer until the polenta is very thick, whisking often, for about 10 minutes. Pour the polenta into the prepared baking pan; spread to a ½-inch (1.3-cm) thick layer. Let it cool completely. When it is cool, use a 1- to 1½-inch (2.5- to 3.8-cm) round cutter to cut as many rounds of polenta as you can. Set aside. Top each round with a small amount of pesto, a chunk of goat cheese and sun-dried tomato. Finish each with a sprinkle of sea salt.

ROASTED CARROTS
WITH SHALLOT AND SAGE

The nutmeg in this recipe really brings out the sweetness of the roasted carrots.
We love to serve this alongside our Apple Cider Braised Chicken (page 168).

SERVES 4 TO 6

---

3 lb (1.5 kg) carrots, peeled

1 cup (240 ml) Chicken Bone Broth
(page 10)

1¼ (6 g) tsp sea salt, we recommend
Selina Naturally Celtic, divided, plus
more

1 tsp cracked pepper, divided, plus more

2 large shallots, thinly sliced

4 tbsp (60 g) unsalted butter

1 small bunch fresh sage, chopped

1 tbsp (3 g) finely chopped thyme

¼ tsp grated nutmeg

Cut the carrots into 3 × ½-inch (7.5 × 1.3-cm) sticks. Bring the bone broth to a boil with ¾ teaspoon salt and a ½ teaspoon pepper in a 12-inch (30.5-cm) skillet. Add the carrots and simmer covered until just tender, about 15 minutes. Remove the lid and boil until most of the liquid has evaporated, about 5 minutes. Transfer the carrots to a bowl and wipe out the skillet. Cook the shallots in butter with ½ teaspoon each of salt and pepper in the skillet over medium heat, stirring occasionally until golden brown, about 6 minutes. Add the sage, thyme and nutmeg, and cook, stirring until very fragrant, 1 to 2 minutes. Remove from the heat and return the carrots to the skillet, tossing to coat. Season with salt and pepper.

PARMESAN AND FENNEL GRATIN

Fennel is such an ironic herb to me. While I can't stand black licorice (which has a very similar flavor profile), there is something I love about roasted fennel bulb that I just can't get enough of. In fact, I will often roast a few handfuls of veggies with an entire fennel in the mix for a quick snack or lunch. This is my kind of potato gratin. I ditch the potatoes and put fennel in its place.

SERVES 4 TO 6

3 medium fennel bulbs

½ cup (120 ml) Chicken Bone Broth (page 10)

⅓ cup (80 ml) dry white wine

Sea salt, we recommend Selina Naturally Celtic

Freshly ground pepper

2 tbsp (30 g) ghee or butter, cubed

3 tbsp (45 ml) ghee or butter, melted

¾ cup (90 g) grain-free bread crumbs

1 cup (180 g) freshly grated Parmesan cheese

1 tbsp (2 g) minced fresh flat-leaf parsley

1½ tsp (5 g) grated lemon zest

Preheat the oven to 375°F (190°C). Remove and discard the stalks from each fennel bulb. Cut the bulbs in half lengthwise through the core. Remove most of the core by cutting a V-shaped wedge, leaving the wedges intact. Cut each piece into 2, 3 or 4 wedges, depending on the size of the bulb. Arrange the wedges cut side up in a gratin dish just large enough to hold them snugly in a single layer. Pour the chicken bone broth and wine over the fennel, then sprinkle with salt and pepper. Dot with the cubed ghee. Cover the dish tightly with aluminum foil and bake for 35 to 45 minutes until the fennel is tender. Remove from the oven and raise the oven temperature to 425°F (220°C). Make the topping by combining the melted ghee grain-free bread crumbs, Parmesan, parsley, zest, 1 teaspoon salt and ½ teaspoon pepper. Sprinkle evenly on top and return to the oven. Bake uncovered for 30 minutes, until the topping is browned.

SAUTÉED FRENCH GREEN BEANS WITH TOASTED ALMONDS

Do you remember the canned green beans your mom or grandma used to serve around Thanksgiving time? They tasted like mush. No wonder we never wanted to eat any vegetables when we were kids! These sautéed fresh French green beans are a side dish that most children will eat when prepared correctly. They have a delicious crunch, and the balsamic vinegar in this recipe hides the "green taste" children complain about with vegetables.

SERVES 4 TO 6

---

1 tbsp (15 g) ghee or butter

1 tbsp (15 ml) extra-virgin olive oil

1 lb (415 g) fresh French green beans, rinsed

1 shallot

1 tbsp (15 g) balsamic vinegar

1 tsp granulated garlic

¼ tsp sea salt, we recommend Selina Naturally Celtic

¼ tsp black pepper

¼ cup (60 ml) Chicken Bone Broth (page 10)

¼ cup (45 g) toasted almonds

In a large sauté pan, warm ghee and olive oil over medium heat until the butter is melted. Add the green beans and sliced shallot. Add the balsamic vinegar and all the seasonings. Toss with tongs and sauté for 5 to 7 minutes. Add the broth and toss with tongs. Cover and cook until desired tenderness is reached. Remove and garnish with almonds.

INDONESIAN PORK SATAY

Skewers are such an easy way to serve protein to a group of people. Finger food is the best! These skewers are great to pack in lunches, too. The dipping sauce has a little bit of sweetness, which calms the red pepper flakes. Children love to dip their food, so this is a great one to serve when you have little visitors.

SERVES 4

2 cloves garlic

½ cup (25 g) green onions, chopped

1 tbsp (15 g) fresh ginger root, chopped

1 cup (150 g) roasted, salted Spanish peanuts

2 tbsp (30 ml) lemon juice

2 tbsp (30 ml) honey

½ cup (120 ml) coconut aminos

2 tsp (4 g) crushed coriander seed

1 tsp crushed red pepper flakes

½ cup (120 ml) Chicken Bone Broth (page 10)

½ cup (120 ml) melted butter

1½ lb (750 g) pork tenderloin, cut into 1-inch (2.5-cm) cubes

Skewers

In a food processor, purée the garlic, green onions, ginger, peanuts, lemon juice, honey, coconut aminos, coriander and red pepper flakes until almost smooth. Pour in the broth and butter, and mix again. Place the pork in a large resealable plastic bag and pour the mixture over the meat. Marinate in the refrigerator for 6 hours or overnight.

Preheat the grill for medium heat. Remove the pork from the bag and thread them onto skewers. In a small saucepan, boil the marinade for 5 minutes. Reserve a small amount of the marinade for basting and set the remainder aside to serve as a dipping sauce. Lightly oil the preheated grill. Grill the skewers for 10 to 15 minutes or until well browned, turning and brushing frequently with the cooked marinade. Serve with the remaining marinade or a dipping sauce of your choice.

COLLARD GREENS WITH BACON

Collard greens tend to be bitter. If you remove the stems from collard greens, you can avoid the bitterness. Adding the bone broth helps to wilt the collard greens, making the texture smooth and palatable, and, of course, bacon makes everything just a little more delicious!

SERVES 4 TO 6

---

1 tbsp (15 ml) extra-virgin olive oil

3 slices bacon

1 large onion, chopped

2 cloves garlic, minced

1 lb (450 g) fresh collard greens, hearts and stems removed, cut into 2-inch (5-cm) pieces

3 cups (720 ml) Chicken Bone Broth (page 10)

1 tsp sea salt, we recommend Selina Naturally Celtic

1 tsp pepper

1 pinch crushed red pepper flakes

Heat the oil in a large pot over medium-high heat. Add the bacon and cook until crisp. Remove the bacon from the pan, crumble and return to the pan. Add the onion and cook until tender, about 5 minutes. Add garlic and cook about 1 minute. Add the collard greens and fry until they start to wilt, about 3 to 5 minutes. Pour in the broth and season with salt, pepper and red pepper flakes. Reduce the heat to low, cover and simmer for 4 to 5 minutes or until the greens are tender.

GREEK LEMON POTATOES

These potatoes are one of our favorite side dishes. We love the tartness of the lemon juice,
and the acidity of this side pairs well with any rich lamb dish.

SERVES 4 TO 6

3 lb (1.5 kg) potatoes, soaked, peeled and cut into wedges

⅓ cup (80 ml) extra-virgin olive oil

2 tbsp (30 g) minced garlic

2 lemons, juiced

2 tsp (10 g) sea salt, we recommend Selina Naturally Celtic

1 tsp oregano

½ tsp ground black pepper

3 cups (720 ml) Chicken Bone Broth (page 10)

Preheat the oven to 400°F (200°C). Put the potato wedges into a large bowl. Combine the olive oil and garlic in a small bowl. Drizzle the olive oil mixture and lemon juice over the wedges and toss to coat. Season the potatoes with salt, oregano and black pepper; toss again to coat. Spread the potato wedges in a single layer in a 2-inch (5-cm) deep pan. Pour the broth over the potatoes. Roast the potatoes until tender and golden brown, about 1 hour.

APPLE AND PECAN RISOTTO WITH GORGONZOLA

Cheese and fruit have been served together for ages. The creamy richness of the gorgonzola pairs well with the sweet-tart quality of the Granny Smith apples. Using bone broth in the place of water for the risotto ensures nourishment while eating this type of carb. This goes well with a delicious grass-fed filet mignon.

SERVES 4 TO 6

---

2 tbsp (30 g) butter, divided

1 green apple, cored and chopped

½ sweet onion, chopped

¾ cup (170 g) arborio rice

1 ½ cups (360 ml) white wine

3 cups (720 ml) Chicken Bone Broth (page 10)

⅓ cup (60 g) gorgonzola cheese

½ cup (60 g) pecans, chopped

Salt and pepper to taste

Chopped parsley, for garnish

Heat a saucepan over medium heat and add 1 tablespoon (15 g) of butter. Add the apple and onion with a pinch of salt and pepper and sauté until soft, about 8 minutes, stirring occasionally. Once soft, add the remaining tablespoon (15 g) of butter, push the apples and onions to the side and add the rice. Toast rice for about 1 minute, then add the wine. Simmer over medium-low heat until the wine is absorbed, about 3 minutes, then add the chicken broth 1 cup (240 ml) at a time, allowing it to be absorbed as well. Stir constantly, making sure nothing is sticking to the bottom. After all the liquid has been added and absorbed, add the gorgonzola and stir until melted. Place the pecans in a small skillet and toast over low heat for about 4 to 5 minutes, occasionally shaking the pan. To serve, top with pecans and parsley.

SWEET POTATO AND KALE QUINOA

For those who add quinoa into their food program, this is a perfect dish. Between the olive oil, kale, bone broth and sweet potatoes, you've got a delicious combination that pairs well with grilled chicken or fish.

SERVES 4 TO 6

---

1 cup (170 g) quinoa

2 cups (480 ml) Chicken Bone Broth (page 10)

2 tbsp (30 ml) extra-virgin olive oil

1 cup (180 g) diced sweet potato

1 cup (100 g) shredded kale

1 cup (50 g) diced carrots

⅓ cup (50 g) diced onions

1 clove garlic

1 tbsp (15 g) butter

Sea salt, to taste, we recommend Selina Naturally Celtic

Cracked black pepper

Place the quinoa into a fine-mesh strainer. Rinse thoroughly with cool water for about 2 minutes. Drain. In a saucepan, add quinoa to the broth and bring to a rolling boil. Lower the heat and cook covered for 15 minutes. Turn the heat down to the lowest setting. Cover and cook for 15 minutes. Remove the pot from the heat and let stand, covered, for 5 minutes. If any liquid remains on the bottom of the pan, then return the pot to low heat and continue to cook until all the liquid is absorbed. Set aside.

In a large skillet, heat the olive oil to medium heat and add all the vegetables except the garlic. Sauté until the vegetables are soft and the onion is translucent. In the last 3 minutes of cooking, add the garlic and butter and sauté. Transfer the cooked quinoa from the saucepan to the skillet and mix the vegetable medley and quinoa well. Salt and pepper to taste.

SWEET POTATO STUFFING

This recipe is always a hit at our holiday parties. Pre-Paleo we would get second and third helpings of stuffing from a box. Those days are long gone! This sweet, salty and savory stuffing will be sure to satisfy that Thanksgiving craving!

SERVES 6 TO 8

1 large yellow onion

4 cloves garlic

3 stalks celery

3 medium sweet potatoes

10 mushrooms

4 tbsp (60 g) butter or ghee

¾ lb (165 g) Italian sausage

8 leaves sage

2 stalks rosemary

8 sprigs thyme

2 tbsp (10 g) organic poultry seasoning

1¾ cups (420 ml) Chicken Bone Broth (page 10)

Salt and pepper, to taste

Dice the onion, garlic and celery. Rinse and peel the sweet potatoes and dice into very small cubes. Chop up the mushrooms and set aside. Add butter and cook up the veggies on medium heat in a pan. Cook for about 10 to 15 minutes or until the veggies start browning or become translucent. In a separate pan, brown the sausage, breaking it into small pieces as you cook. Combine the sausage, veggie mix, herbs, poultry seasoning, mushrooms and broth, and cook down for a few minutes. Add salt and pepper. Put the mixture in a glass baking dish and bake at 350°F (180°C) for roughly an hour, stirring at about the halfway point. The stuffing will be done when the potatoes mash up slightly when stirred.

BRAISED CABBAGE WITH APPLE AND BACON

Bacon really elevates the cabbage in this dish! The sweetness of the apple and saltiness of the bacon will have even your pickiest eaters coming back for seconds.

SERVES 6 TO 8

4 thick slices of bacon, cut into ¼-inch (6-mm) pieces

4 celery hearts, thinly sliced

1 medium onion, thinly sliced

½ cup (120 ml) white wine

1 head red cabbage, thinly sliced

1 cup (240 ml) Chicken Bone Broth (page 10)

1 cup (240 ml) unfiltered apple cider

1 garlic clove, thinly sliced

2 bay leaves

1 tart apple, thinly sliced

Salt and pepper, to taste

1 tbsp (15 ml) apple cider vinegar

Cook the bacon in a Dutch oven over medium heat until crisp. Remove the bacon from the pan and drain the bacon fat, keeping 3 tablespoons (45 ml) of the drippings in the pan. Increase the heat to medium-high. Add the celery and onion, and sauté 5 minutes. Add the white wine and cook 2 minutes or until reduced by half. Stir in the cabbage and all remaining ingredients except the vinegar. Add salt and pepper. Reduce the heat to low. Cover and cook 45 minutes. Stir in the vinegar. Top with bacon and serve.

GOAT CHEESE GOUDA
AND GARLIC MASHED CAULIFLOWER

Mashed potatoes are an all-American food! But they can be boring after a while. This Gouda mashed cauliflower captures that creamy, buttery, rich decadence of mashed potatoes while using a vegetable that is Paleo-compliant and seriously delicious!

SERVES 4 TO 6

5 cups (1.1 kg) cauliflower florets

2 tbsp (30 g) butter or ghee

2 cloves of garlic, minced well

2 tbsp (30 ml) Chicken Bone Broth (page 10)

2 tbsp (30 ml) heavy cream or coconut cream

½ tsp sea salt, we recommend Selina Naturally Celtic

¼ tsp black pepper

⅓ cup (40 g) shredded smoked Gouda

Salt and pepper to taste

Place a steamer insert into a saucepan and fill with water to just below the bottom of the steamer. Bring the water to a boil. Add the cauliflower, cover and steam until tender, about 10 minutes.

Meanwhile, heat the butter in a small skillet over medium heat. Add the garlic, cooking and stirring until softened, about 2 minutes. Remove from the heat. Transfer half the cauliflower to a food processor; cover and blend on high. Add the remaining cauliflower florets one at a time until they are creamy. Add in the garlic, broth, cream, salt and black pepper, and blend until creamy. Add the smoked Gouda. Blend until smooth. Transfer to a bowl and season with additional salt and pepper if needed.

SAUTÉED MUSHROOM, ASPARAGUS AND ONION MEDLEY

This side dish is one of our favorite quickies on busy weekday nights. The delicious crunch of the asparagus brings texture to the mushrooms and onions. We love it served on top of steak or it can be served alongside any of your other favorite proteins.

SERVES 6 TO 8

½ cup (120 ml) extra-virgin olive oil

1 bunch of asparagus cut into 1-inch (2.5-cm) pieces

1 (10-oz [280-g]) container cremini mushrooms, diced

1 large leek, chopped

1 yellow onion, sliced

1 shallot, diced

3 cloves of garlic, minced

Sea salt, we recommend Selina Naturally Celtic

Pepper

Garlic powder

¼ cup (60 ml) Chicken Bone Broth (page 10)

Heat a sauté pan with the olive oil on medium heat. Add all the vegetables, garlic, salt, pepper and garlic powder and stir. Sauté for 5 minutes until the onions are soft. Add the broth and deglaze the pan. Turn down the heat to medium-low and let simmer, stirring occasionally, for 10 minutes or until most of the liquid evaporates.

CHILLED AVOCADO SOUP WITH ADOBO SHRIMP

We are big soup lovers, but what do we do when it's blazing hot outside and we're craving soup? Make a chilled soup, of course! The avocado gives this a natural creaminess without dairy, and the heat of the adobo shrimp and fresh cilantro bring a brightness to the dish that balances the flavors perfectly.

SERVES 6 TO 8

3 cups (720 ml) Chicken Bone Broth (page 10)

2 avocados, peeled and diced

2 tbsp (5 g) fresh cilantro, chopped, plus more to serve

2 tbsp (30 ml) fresh lime juice

¼ tsp sea salt, we recommend Selina Naturally Celtic

¼ tsp freshly ground black pepper

1 lb (450 g) medium shrimp, peeled and deveined

¼ tsp cumin

½ tsp freshly ground black pepper

¼ tsp sea salt, we recommend Selina Naturally Celtic

1 (7-oz [200-g]) can chilies in adobo sauce

Coconut oil

¼ cup (40 g) red onion, finely chopped

1 garlic clove, minced

1 tbsp (15 ml) fresh lime juice, plus more

To make the adobo sauce, place the chicken broth, avocados, cilantro, lime juice, salt and pepper in a blender or food processor, and purée until smooth. Cover and chill.

Sprinkle the shrimp with cumin, pepper, salt and set aside. Remove 1 tablespoon (15 ml) of adobo sauce from the can and set aside. Heat a large nonstick skillet over medium-high heat and coat with coconut oil. Add the shrimp and cook 4 minutes, flipping halfway. Add the onion and garlic, and sauté for 2 minutes. Add the reserved adobo sauce and lime juice. Sauté for 2 minutes or until shrimp are cooked through and vegetables are crisp-tender. Top with lime juice, shrimp and cilantro and serve.

BUTTERNUT SQUASH "MAC AND CHEESE"

Creamy, rich, decadent. This butternut squash macaroni and cheese is all three of those things! One of the biggest missed foods for Paleo kids is good ol' macaroni and cheese. This recipe was given to us by one of our clients, and when we tried it, we couldn't believe how delicious it was! The creaminess of the butternut squash gives it that satisfying texture that we love about traditional macaroni and cheese. This is one of those nights that you go off your eating plan and go for some quinoa pasta or rice pasta.

SERVES 6 TO 8

1 butternut squash

1 tbsp (15 ml) extra-virgin olive oil

¼ tsp sea salt, plus more, we recommend Selina Naturally Celtic

Pinch of freshly ground pepper

2 tbsp (30 g) butter, unsalted

½ cup (75 g) yellow onion, diced

1 tsp fresh thyme, minced

¼ tsp ground nutmeg

½ cup (120 ml) heavy raw cream or coconut cream

½ cup (120 ml) Chicken Bone Broth (page 10)

1 cup (180 g) shaved pecorino (sheep's milk) cheese, plus additional for topping

3 cups (350 g) organic, gluten-free (quinoa) pasta shells

Thyme sprig, for garnish

Preheat the oven to 425°F (220°C). Peel, seed and cut the butternut squash into 1-inch (2.5-cm) cubes and place them in a large mixing bowl. Add the olive oil to the mixing bowl along with a pinch of salt and pepper; stir to combine. Cover a baking sheet with foil and spread the squash on it in a single layer. Roast for 35 to 45 minutes, turning once halfway through the roasting time. Remove the butternut squash from the oven and reduce the heat to 375°F (190°C). Allow the squash to cool to room temperature. Place it in a food processor and pulse until smooth.

Meanwhile, in a large saucepan over medium heat, melt the butter. Add the onion to the pan and sauté for 5 minutes or until translucent. Remove the pan from the heat and add the thyme, nutmeg and salt to the onion mixture, stirring to combine. Place the pan back on the burner over medium heat, add the butternut squash purée, coconut cream and the broth, stirring constantly. Add the pecorino cheese and stir continuously until melted. Remove from the heat and set aside.

Meanwhile, bring 1 quart (1 L) of salted water to a boil in a large saucepan. Cook the gluten-free pasta according to package instructions to al dente texture. Drain and place cooked macaroni in a 9 × 9-inch (23 × 23-cm) casserole dish. Pour the butternut squash cheese sauce over the pasta and stir to combine. Top with a sprinkle of pecorino cheese and bake the mac and cheese for 15 to 20 minutes or until the cheese has melted. Let cool for 5 minutes after baking and serve topped with a thyme sprig.

ASPARAGUS WITH CITRUS AND CHIVE CREAM

This side dish is a perfect complement to a fillet of wild-caught salmon or sea bass. The brightness of the lemon and chives pairs perfectly with the rich cream cheese and creates a side dish that is perfect for summer night dinners.

SERVES 4 TO 6

2 lb (900 g) fresh asparagus spears, trimmed

1 tbsp (15 ml) water

Pinch of sea salt, we recommend Selina Naturally Celtic

¼ cup (60 ml) Chicken Bone Broth (page 10)

½ cup (120 g) cream cheese

½ tsp lemon zest

½ tbsp (1.5 g) fresh chives, chopped, plus more for garnishing

Place the asparagus in a steamer basket over a sauce pan with 1 inch (2.5 cm) of water and a pinch of salt. Cover and steam until very tender. Meanwhile, heat the broth in a small saucepan. Add the cream cheese and cook, stirring constantly until melted and the sauce is slightly thickened. Stir in the zest and chives. Spoon the cream mixture over the asparagus, garnish with chopped chives to serve.

CRISPY BONE BROTH POTATOES

One of our all-time favorite side dishes is crispy baby potatoes. My sister makes these at least once a week, and they always have us coming back for seconds. The broth cooks the inside of the potatoes to a fluffy, delicious texture, while the last step in the skillet gives them a salty, satisfying crunch!

SERVES 4 TO 6

1½ lb (680 g) organic baby potatoes

1 sprig rosemary

3 sprigs thyme

2 cups (480 ml) Chicken Bone Broth (page 10), plus ½ cup (120 ml), if needed

2 tbsp (30 ml) extra-virgin olive oil

2 tbsp (30 g) butter or ghee, divided

1 tsp sea salt, we recommend Selina Naturally Celtic, plus more for topping

2 cloves garlic, minced

In a large nonstick skillet, arrange the baby potatoes so that they fit together neatly but with a bit of extra room. Add the rosemary, thyme, 2 cups (480 ml) broth, olive oil, 1 tablespoon (15 g) butter and salt. Heat the pan to high and bring to a boil. Once the broth boils, reduce the heat to medium, add in the garlic and cover the skillet halfway, leaving a small space for excess steam to escape. Continue to boil the broth and potatoes for about 20 minutes or until the potatoes can be easily pierced with a fork. If the liquid has all absorbed, add the additional ½ cup (120 ml) of the broth. Remove the pan from the heat and use a wooden spoon to push down on the tops of the potatoes lightly until the skin cracks and they flatten out a bit. Return the potatoes to high heat and cook uncovered until the liquid evaporates and the potatoes are browned on the bottom, about 12 minutes. Remove the skillet from the heat again, turn the potatoes, scrape up any burned bits and add the remaining tablespoon (15 g) of butter to the pan. Press the other sides of the potatoes to crack and flatten them more if necessary. Cook until the other side is browned, about 5 minutes. Serve warm and sprinkled with salt.

ARUGULA, PARMESAN AND PEA SPROUTED RISOTTO

I love how the bone broth in this recipe really balances out the flavor of the wine. No boring rice here; just an explosion of flavor in every bite. The key to any great risotto is to stir as often as you can. Risotto must be tended to. It's a labor of love. While we don't eat a lot of rice, this is one dish we crave.

SERVES 4 TO 6

---

1 tbsp (15 g) butter

1 tbsp (15 ml) extra-virgin olive oil

¼ cup (40 g) minced shallot

2 leeks, thinly sliced

2 cups (450 g) risotto

½ cup (120 ml) dry white wine

4 cups (960 ml) Chicken Bone Broth (page 10), divided

1 cup (150 g) frozen organic peas

2 cups (200 g) organic fresh arugula

1 cup (180 g) freshly grated Parmesan cheese, plus more

Salt and pepper to taste

3 to 4 slices cooked, crumbled bacon pieces

Heat the butter and oil in a large pot over medium heat. Add the shallot and leeks and cook, stirring occasionally until they are soft and translucent, about 5 minutes. Add the risotto and stir until the grains are coated with the oil and butter. Add the wine and simmer until it is almost completely absorbed. Add 1 cup (240 ml) of warmed broth to the risotto. Simmer gently and stir occasionally until the broth is almost absorbed. Continue to add broth in 1-cup (240-ml) increments until all the broth has been used and the risotto is tender and creamy, around 20 minutes. During the last 5 minutes of cooking, stir in the peas. The heat from the risotto should cook them sufficiently. When the risotto is done, stir in the arugula one handful at a time until it is wilted. Stir in the cheese and taste for seasoning, adding salt and pepper if necessary. Serve the risotto immediately in wide bowls topped with additional Parmesan cheese and bacon.

CARAMELIZED ONION
AND SWEET POTATO STACKS

This side dish is not only visually beautiful but the tender, sweet and savory flavors of the caramelized onion and sweet potato go perfectly together. Earthy, fresh thyme ties all of these flavors together in a side dish that is sure to impress.

SERVES 4 TO 6

2 tbsp (30 ml) extra-virgin olive oil

3 brown onions, thickly sliced

1 lb (450 g) sweet potatoes, peeled and thinly sliced

⅔ cup (160 ml) Chicken Bone Broth (page 10)

5½ tbsp (82 ml) butter or ghee, melted

8 sprigs thyme

Preheat the oven to 350°F (180°C). Heat the oil in a large frying pan over medium heat. Add the onion slices and cook in batches for 3 minutes or until golden. Place an onion slice in the bottom of eight ½-cup (120-ml) muffin cups lined with parchment paper. Layer with potato slices and finish with a slice of onion. Divide the stock and butter among the stacks and top with a thyme sprig. Cover with foil and bake for 30 minutes. Remove the foil and bake for another 30 minutes or until the onions and potatoes are cooked through and golden.

CREAMY MASHED CARROTS AND SWEET POTATOES

This dish goes perfectly with our Apple Cider Braised Chicken (page 168). The sweetness of the carrots and nutmeg are a nod to our favorite fall flavors. We like to serve this with an extra pat of grass-fed butter.

SERVES 4 TO 6

⅓ cup (80 ml) extra-virgin olive oil

1 large onion, diced

3 cloves garlic, minced

2 lb (300 g) organic carrots, thinly sliced

2 lb (900 g) sweet potatoes, ends trimmed, peeled and cut into 1-inch (2.5-cm) pieces

1 tsp sea salt, plus extra for seasoning, we recommend Selina Naturally Celtic

1 tsp nutmeg

½ tsp freshly ground black pepper, plus extra for seasoning

4 cups (960 ml) Chicken Bone Broth (page 10)

½ cup (120 ml) water

In a saucepan or Dutch oven, heat the oil over medium-high heat. Add the onion and cook until tender, about 5 minutes. Add the garlic and cook for 1 minute. Add the carrots, sweet potatoes, 1 teaspoon salt, nutmeg and ½ teaspoon pepper. Cook until slightly softened, about 5 to 7 minutes. Add the broth and water and bring to a boil. Reduce the heat and simmer until the carrots are tender, about 20 minutes. Using a ladle, remove 2 cups (480 ml) of the cooking liquid and set aside. In a blender, blend the mixture until slightly chunky, adding the reserved cooking liquid, ¼ cup (60 ml) at a time, if needed. Season with salt and pepper to taste.

BONE BROTH RATATOUILLE

When you have leftover vegetables lying around in the fridge, ratatouille is an excellent option!
We always have leftover zucchini, onions and squash from breakfast scrambles, so throwing this together
for dinner is a breeze. Its mild flavor complements nearly any protein you serve with it!

SERVES 4 TO 6

2 tbsp (30 ml) extra-virgin olive oil

1 large red onion, ½-inch (1.3-cm) dice

2 cloves garlic, finely chopped

½ cup (60 g) toasted pine nuts

½ cup (120 ml) Chicken Bone Broth (page 10)

1 medium eggplant, ½-inch (1.3-cm) dice

2 large, ripe tomatoes, diced

2 small zucchini, ½-inch (1.3-cm) dice

2 small yellow squash, ½-inch (1.3-cm) dice

1½ tsp (3 g) dried oregano

Heat a heavy-bottomed sauté pan over medium heat for a minute; once hot, add the oil. When the oil is hot, add the onion, garlic and pine nuts and sauté for 3 minutes or until the onion is slightly soft. Add the broth and eggplant and cook, stirring occasionally, for about 10 minutes or until the eggplant is tender. Add the tomatoes, zucchini and yellow squash, and cook for about 10 more minutes or until the zucchini and squash are tender but still firm to the bite and brightly colored. Stir in the oregano about a minute before cooking is finished.

SAUSAGE, ONION AND PEPPER POTATOES

We come from a German family, so we know a little something about onions, sausage and potatoes. This side dish is one of our favorites to make because not only is it packed with protein, but also because the bell peppers and sautéed onions give it a delicious sweetness and crunch that can't be beat.

SERVES 4 TO 6

2 tsp (10 ml) + ¼ cup (60 ml) extra-virgin olive oil, divided

2 lb (900 g) Italian sausage links, cut into 2-inch (5-cm) pieces

4 large soaked potatoes, peeled and thickly sliced

2 large green bell peppers, seeded and cut into wedges

2 large red bell peppers, seeded and cut into wedges

3 large onions, cut into wedges

½ cup (120 ml) white wine (optional, if decided against, substitute with Chicken Bone Broth [page 10])

½ cup (120 ml) Chicken Bone Broth (page 10)

1 tsp Italian seasoning

Salt and pepper, to taste

Preheat the oven to 400°F (200°C). Heat 2 teaspoons (10 ml) of oil in a large skillet over medium heat. Add the sausage and cook until browned. Transfer the cooked sausage to a large baking dish. Pour ¼ cup (60 ml) of olive oil into the skillet and cook the potatoes, stirring occasionally until browned, about 10 minutes. Place the potatoes into the baking dish, leaving some oil. Cook the green and red peppers and onions in the hot skillet, stirring occasionally, until they are beginning to soften, about 5 minutes. Add the vegetables to the baking dish. Pour wine and broth over the vegetables and sausage, and sprinkle with Italian seasoning, salt and pepper. Gently stir the sausage, potatoes and vegetables together. Bake until hot and bubbling, about 20 to 25 minutes. Serve hot.

BONAFIDE SOUPS

Soups are one of the easiest meals to ensure better health. However, making soup with a canned broth or stock may add extra sodium, flavors and MSG to your healthy diet. Make your own bone broth and use it as a base for any soup. You can rotate vegetables, proteins and a variety of herbs into most recipes to ensure you are getting vitamins, minerals and nutrients from your food. Soups should be rotated into your breakfast routine a few times per week. You can make large batches of soup, refrigerate them in freezer-safe mason jars and grab them for either breakfast or lunch. The rich bone broth base in the soup ensures you are getting the extra minerals, amino acids and nutrients in your meal.

ROASTED BUTTERNUT SQUASH SOUP

Roasted Butternut Squash Soup is one of our favorite fall and winter meals. It's rich, creamy and soothing on cold winter nights. We love that this recipe doesn't require any cream. Instead, we've used chicken bone broth to blend together the sweet and savory flavors!

SERVES 4 TO 6

---

2 tbsp (30 g) butter

1 small onion, chopped

1 stalk celery, chopped

1 medium carrot, chopped

1 medium sweet potato, cubed

1 medium butternut squash, peeled, seeded and cubed

4 cups (960 ml) Chicken Bone Broth (page 10)

Salt and freshly ground black pepper, to taste

Melt the butter in a large pot and cook the onion, celery, carrot, sweet potato and squash for 5 minutes, or until lightly browned. Pour in enough of the broth to cover the vegetables. Bring to a boil. Reduce the heat to low, cover the pot and simmer 40 minutes or until all the vegetables are tender. Transfer the soup to a blender and blend until smooth. Return the vegetables to the pot and mix in any remaining broth to attain desired consistency. Season with salt and pepper.

SPRING PEA SOUP WITH CRISPY PANCETTA

Ham and peas have long been a staple flavor combination. We elevated it by adding deliciously crispy,
salty pancetta. The pancetta pairs perfectly with the sweet, creamy texture of spring peas.
We love to top ours with lots of fresh cracked pepper and sea salt.

SERVES 4 TO 6

2 tbsp (30 ml) extra-virgin olive oil +
½ tbsp (7.5 ml)

½ cup (75 g) shallots, chopped

1 tbsp (5 g) garlic, minced

4 cups (960 ml) Chicken Bone Broth
(page 10)

2 lb (900 g) frozen organic peas

2 tsp (10 g) sea salt, we recommend
Selina Naturally Celtic

1 tsp freshly ground black pepper

1 cup (225 g) diced pancetta

In a deep heavy-bottomed saucepan, heat 2 tablespoons (30 ml) of the olive oil over medium heat. Add the shallots and sauté for 3 to 5 minutes stirring until tender and lightly browned. Add the garlic and cook for 1 more minute. Add the broth, frozen peas, salt and pepper and bring to a boil. Lower the heat and simmer for 5 minutes. Use either a blender or immersion blender to purée well. Pour the soup back into the pot and season to taste. In a separate sauté pan over medium heat, add the remaining ½ tablespoon (7.5 ml) oil and pancetta. Stir well. Cook until the pancetta is crispy, browned and thoroughly cooked, about 5 to 7 minutes. Remove from the heat and transfer the pancetta to a paper towel–lined plate to drain. To serve, ladle the soup into a bowl and top with crispy pancetta.

SPRING PEA AND COCONUT MILK SOUP

We love Thai-inspired flavors, so this soup is an absolute favorite in our home. The fragrant, spicy ginger and rich, creamy coconut milk create a soup that has incredible flavor depth. Coconut milk is a great source of antiviral, antibacterial lauric acid. Pairing it with the fresh flavors of cilantro and lime juice makes for a winning combination.

SERVES 4 TO 6

1 tbsp (15 g) coconut oil

½ white onion, peeled and roughly chopped

1 large clove garlic

1 tbsp (15 g) fresh ginger, peeled and minced

1 bunch cilantro, leaves and stems separated and roughly chopped

4 cups (960 ml) Chicken Bone Broth (page 10)

1 tbsp (15 ml) fish sauce

1 (14-oz [395-ml]) can full-fat coconut milk

2 (12-oz [340-g]) bags frozen, shelled peas

1 medium lime, juiced

Heat the coconut oil in a large pot over medium heat. Add the chopped onion, garlic, ginger and the stems of the cilantro to the coconut oil. Cook until the onion is tender and translucent, about 5 to 7 minutes. Add the bone broth, fish sauce and coconut milk to the onion mixture. Bring all to a simmer. Add frozen peas and cook until tender but still bright green, about 4 minutes. Add in the lime juice and half the chopped cilantro leaves; reserve half for garnish. Remove soup from the heat just after adding the lime and cilantro, and purée the soup with an immersion blender until smooth. Garnish with reserved cilantro and lime and serve.

FRENCH ONION SOUP

We grew up in a generation that was used to eating French onion soup from a powdered mix. No more of that! You won't even miss the croutons in this Paleo version. The beef bone broth base is rich in flavor, and the slightly salty, nutty flavor of the grass-fed Gruyère cheese complements the sweet onions.

SERVES 4 TO 6

4 tbsp (60 g) butter, ghee or bacon fat

7 cups (600 g) yellow onion, sliced thinly into half circles

4 cups (960 ml) Beef Bone Broth (page 11)

2 tbsp (6 g) fresh thyme leaves

1 tsp sea salt, we recommend Selina Naturally Celtic

Pepper to taste

10 oz (280 g) grass-fed Gruyère cheese, grated or very thinly sliced

Heat the butter in a large saucepan over medium heat. Add the onion slices and cook until they reduce to half their original size. Stir frequently to prevent burning while allowing the onions to brown. Add the bone broth and scrape the bottom of the pan. Add the thyme, salt and pepper, stir and bring to a simmer. Simmer for 5 minutes. Pour the soup while still hot into small 1-cup (237-ml) bowls or ramekins, top with Gruyère cheese and set under the broiler at 400°F (200°C) for 2 to 3 minutes or until golden brown.

ROASTED GARLIC AND PARSNIP SOUP

I think what makes this soup so wonderful is the roasted parsnips, onion and garlic. I can make this soup a side dish on its own. Don't be afraid to try a garlic soup. When roasted, the garlic becomes sweet and the maple syrup really complements the roasted garlic well.

SERVES 4 TO 6

1½ lb (750 g) parsnips, peeled and chopped

1 brown onion, peeled and chopped

3 bulbs roasted garlic

1 tbsp (15 ml) extra-virgin olive oil

Sea salt, we recommend Selina Naturally Celtic

Cracked black pepper, plus more for serving

2 tbsp (30 ml) organic, grade B maple syrup

6½ cups (1.5 L) Chicken Bone Broth (page 10)

¼ cup (60 g) sour cream

Preheat the oven to 395°F (200°C). Toss the parsnips, onion and garlic bulbs in olive oil, salt and pepper and place on a baking sheet. Roast for 20 minutes. Drizzle with the maple syrup and cook for 10 minutes more or until tender. Place the parsnips, onion and broth in a medium saucepan; squeeze the garlic from the skin of 2 of the bulbs and add it to the saucepan. Using a handheld immersion blender, blend until smooth. Place over high heat, stir in the sour cream and cook for 2 minutes. Squeeze the remaining garlic from the skin and stir through the soup. Garnish with fresh cracked pepper to serve.

EGG DROP SOUP

This is one of our favorite breakfast soups. It's packed with protein and quality fats, and the mild flavor is perfect for a soothing meal in the morning, afternoon or evening.

SERVES 4 TO 6

4 cups (960 ml) Chicken Bone Broth (page 10)

1 tbsp (15 g) arrowroot

1 tsp ground ginger

¼ tsp garlic powder

2 large organic eggs

2 large organic egg whites

½ tsp sesame oil

3 green onions, sliced thin, plus extra for garnish

Sea salt to taste, we recommend Selina Naturally Celtic

Black pepper, to taste

Whisk together the chicken broth (chilled or at room temperature), arrowroot, ginger and garlic powder in a medium saucepan until combined and no lumps remain. Heat over high heat until boiling, stirring occasionally. Meanwhile, whisk together the eggs and egg whites in a small measuring cup or bowl. Once the broth reaches a boil, remove it from the heat. Then use a fork or whisk to stir the broth in a circular motion while slowly pouring the whisked eggs into the soup to create egg ribbons. Stir in the sesame oil and green onions until combined. Season with salt and pepper to taste and top with green onions.

HOMEMADE CONDENSED CREAM OF CHICKEN AND MUSHROOM SOUP

When I was a child, the trend was to add cream of mushroom soup to green beans. This soup is nothing like that old canned standby. I have actually used this soup as a sauce on top of my grilled chicken breasts!

SERVES 8 TO 10

3 medium onions, coarsely chopped

4 tbsp (60 g) butter

Pinch sea salt, we recommend Selina Naturally Celtic, plus more to taste

1 cup (70 g) cremini mushrooms, steupms removed and diced

5 cloves garlic, coarsely chopped

8 cups (2 L) Chicken Bone Broth (page 10)

2 tbsp (10 g) organic poultry seasoning

2 tsp (1 g) parsley

¼ tsp paprika

6 cups (1.5 L) coconut milk or raw milk

1½ cups (230 g) organic white rice flour

Sauté the onions in butter with a pinch of salt and the mushrooms for 5 to 7 minutes to soften. Add the garlic and cook for a minute. Add the broth and poultry seasoning, parsley and paprika, and bring to a boil. Reduce to a simmer for a few minutes. Remove from heat. Using an immersion blender, blend the onions well into the stock. A regular blender can be used as well. Bring the soup back up to a simmer while you whisk together the coconut milk and flour in a mixing bowl until it is a well-combined slurry. Add the slurry mixture to the simmering soup and continue to whisk well for 7 to 10 minutes.

ITALIAN SAUSAGE SOUP

This is a recipe we served in our restaurant. It is super-easy to whip together and can be a meal all by itself. The tomatoes give it an acidic kick, while the carrots, zucchini and Italian sausage bring a naturally sweet and salty balance.

SERVES 4 TO 6

1 lb (450 g) Italian sausage

1 clove garlic, minced

2 cups (480 ml) Beef Bone Broth (page 11)

1 (14-oz [395-g]) can Italian-style stewed tomatoes

1 cup (120 g) carrots, sliced

¼ tsp sea salt, we recommend Selina Naturally Celtic

¼ tsp ground black pepper

2 small zucchini, cubed

2 cups (60 g) spinach, packed, rinsed and torn

In a stockpot or Dutch oven, brown the sausage with the garlic. Stir in the broth, tomatoes and carrots, and season with salt and pepper. Reduce the heat, cover and simmer for 15 minutes.

Stir in the zucchini. Cover and simmer for another 15 minutes or until the zucchini is tender. Remove from the heat, add spinach and cover, allowing the heat from the soup to cook the spinach leaves. The soup is ready to serve after 5 minutes.

RAW CHEDDAR AND BROCCOLI SOUP

This is a really healthy version of this old classic. No guilt here when eating this soup.
You can always substitute coconut milk for the raw milk if you aren't doing dairy.

SERVES 6 TO 8

3 tbsp (45 g) butter or ghee

1 large carrot, shredded

1 large shallot, chopped

Sea salt to taste, we recommend Selina Naturally Celtic

Freshly cracked pepper

3 cups (720 ml) Chicken Bone Broth (page 10)

1 cup (240 ml) raw milk

1 cup (240 ml) raw heavy cream

3 cups (525 g) fresh broccoli florets, chopped small

8 oz (227 g) raw shredded sharp cheddar cheese, plus more for serving

Melt the butter in a large soup pot or Dutch oven over medium heat, then add the carrot and shallot, season with salt and pepper and sauté until the carrots are tender, about 3 to 5 minutes. Pour in the chicken broth and heat. Add the milk and cream, season with salt and pepper and increase heat to medium-high to bring the soup to a simmer. Turn the heat to medium, then simmer for 10 minutes, stirring occasionally. Add the broccoli florets to the pot and cover to simmer for 20 more minutes or until the broccoli is tender. Remove the pot from the heat, then add cheese in three batches, stirring until it's completely smooth before adding the next batch. For a thinner soup, mash broccoli with a potato masher or leave in whole pieces. Serve with fresh raw cheddar on top and fresh cracked pepper.

COCONUT CURRY AND LIME SOUP

I always have to sing that old song, "You put the lime in the coconut and drink it all up" when I make this soup. My kids think I'm nutty, but that is okay. So go ahead, sing along with me when you make this soup. There is a reason a song was made about this combination. They pair well!

SERVES 4 TO 6

2 (13.5-oz [398-ml]) cans organic, coconut milk

I heaping tbsp (16 g) Thai curry paste

I bunch cilantro leaves, rinsed well, 2 stems, set aside

2 chicken breasts, thinly sliced

2 cups (480 ml) Chicken Bone Broth (page 10)

3 carrots, shredded

5 lime leaves

2 stalks lemon grass, halved lengthwise, woody leaves removed

2 tbsp (30 ml) fish sauce

I tbsp (6 g) fresh grated ginger

I tbsp (6 g) lime zest

2 limes, juiced

I cup (100 g) bean sprouts

½ tbsp (7 ml) coconut aminos

Scoop the thick coconut cream from the top of just one of the cans into a large stockpot set over a medium-high heat. Melt the cream, add the curry paste and stir for a few minutes until it begins to sizzle. Add the cilantro stems and chicken and sauté until the chicken is cooked through, about 5 minutes. Add the coconut milk from the first can and all the contents of the second can along with the broth, carrots, lime leaves, lemon grass, fish sauce, ginger and lime zest and juice. Simmer for 20 minutes or so. Stir in the bean sprouts and half of the cilantro leaves. Season to taste with coconut aminos. To serve, ladle into a bowl and top with remaining cilantro leaves.

GREEK LEMON SOUP WITH RICE

This is a really easy soup to make. As long as you have your soaked rice prepared ahead of time, you can throw this together in a snap. The fresh lemon adds a kick, and I love the creaminess that the egg brings to the dish.

SERVES 4 TO 6

3½ cups (840 ml) Chicken Bone Broth (page 10)

¼ cup (46 g) long-grain rice, rinsed

2 cloves garlic, minced

⅓ cup (78 ml) fresh lemon juice

1 large organic egg, lightly beaten

2 tbsp (7 g) fresh parsley, finely chopped

Sea salt to taste, we recommend Selina Naturally Celtic

White pepper, to taste (optional)

Heat the broth to a boil in a medium saucepan, then stir in the rice and garlic. Reduce the heat and simmer, covered, until the rice is tender, about 25 minutes. Reduce the heat to low. Mix the lemon juice and egg together, and slowly stir mixture into the soup. Stir in the parsley and season to taste with salt and white pepper, if using. Pour the soup into bowls and serve.

CIOPPINO

When we put this dish on our menu in our restaurant, it would often sell out. It's one of our favorite dishes on a cold winter night. This rich, hearty, seafood stew is even better when you use real bone broth. The rich saltiness of the seafood is complemented by the acidity of the stewed tomatoes. Be sure to have some Paleo bread handy to dip into the soup and soak up all of the delicious leftover broth.

SERVES 4 TO 6

¾ cup (170 g) butter

2 onions, chopped

2 cloves garlic, minced

1 bunch fresh parsley, chopped

2 (14½-oz [395-g]) cans stewed tomatoes

4 cups (960 ml) Chicken Bone Broth (page 10)

2 bay leaves

1 tbsp (5 g) dried basil

½ tsp dried thyme

½ tsp dried oregano

1 cup (240 ml) water

1½ cups (360 ml) white wine

1½ lb (675 g) large shrimp, peeled and deveined

1½ lb (675 g) bay scallops

18 small clams

18 mussels, cleaned and debearded

1½ cups (135 g) crabmeat

1½ lb (675 g) cod fillets, cubed (optional)

Over medium-low heat, melt the butter in a large stockpot, then add the onions, garlic and parsley. Cook slowly, stirring occasionally until the onions are soft. Add tomatoes to the pot (break them into chunks as you add them). Add the chicken broth, bay leaves, basil, thyme, oregano, water and wine. Mix well. Cover and simmer for 30 minutes. Stir in the shrimp, scallops, clams, mussels and crabmeat. Stir in the cod, if using. Bring to a boil. Lower the heat, cover and simmer for 5 to 7 minutes or until the clams open.

ROASTED TOMATO BASIL SOUP

This is the perfect soup to serve with Paleo bread grilled cheese sandwiches. My kids love to dip
the sandwich into the soup. You can leave the dash of red pepper flakes out if your kids don't like it spicy. Of
course, make extra for midweek dinners. You will find that making this old standby
with real bone broth adds a totally new depth to this soup.

SERVES 4 TO 6

2½ lb (1.2 kg) organic Roma tomatoes, halved

4 tbsp (60 ml) extra-virgin olive oil, divided

Sea salt to taste, we recommend Selina Naturally Celtic

Freshly cracked pepper

1 medium onion, chopped

4 cloves of garlic, minced

Dash of crushed red pepper flakes

1 (15-oz [425-g]) can organic diced tomatoes

1 cup (40 g) basil, freshly chopped, plus more for topping

4 cups (960 ml) Chicken Bone Broth (page 10)

Preheat the oven to 400°F (200°C). Spread the tomatoes on a baking sheet and drizzle with 2 tablespoons (30 ml) of olive oil. Season with salt and pepper and roast for about 45 minutes. Remove from the oven and set aside.

In a large stockpot, heat the remaining 2 tablespoons (30 ml) of olive oil over medium heat. Add the onion and cook until tender, about 2 to 3 minutes. Stir in the garlic and red pepper flakes. Cook for another 2 to 3 minutes. Add the canned tomatoes, basil and broth. Stir in the oven-roasted tomatoes. Cook for about 30 minutes over medium-low heat. Use an immersion blender to purée the soup in the stockpot or transfer the soup to a food processor or blender to blend. Purée until almost completely smooth or leave some chunks to add texture to your soup. Top with fresh basil and cracked pepper and serve.

See photo on page 80.

COMFORT FOODS FOR ALL OCCASIONS

There is nothing more comforting than a meal that reminds you of joyful memories. The delicious smells, tastes and textures can be a reminder of good meals with great friends, precious holiday dinners spent with family or even just time spent with people you love. These are some of our favorite comfort foods, and we've elevated the flavor by using real bone broth. Now your old favorites can be your nutrient-dense favorites, too. Not only are they dear to our hearts but also they have flavor that will blow your mind. Enjoy!

GRAIN-FREE CHICKEN POT PIE

I may be dating myself but do you remember the frozen pot pies you had for dinner as a kid? I always picked the peas out because I hated any type of vegetable. My taste buds have really transformed over time (thankfully), but my desire for pot pie never has. This is a version that we make in our home, and it's a great meal to serve on cold winter nights. Make extra and freeze for quick meals during the week. You are going to love the crust on this one. It is flaky and there is enough to get a little crust in every bite.

SERVES 4 TO 6

THE CRUST

1½ cups (145 g) blanched almond flour

½ cup (60 g) tapioca flour

1 tsp sea salt, we recommend Selina Naturally Celtic

½ tsp baking powder

⅔ cup (150 g) organic palm shortening

6 tbsp (90 ml) cold water

THE FILLING

4 tbsp (60 g) butter

½ cup (75 g) onion, finely diced

½ cup (65 g) carrot, finely diced

½ cup (50 g) celery, finely diced

3 cups (375 g) cooked chicken, shredded

¼ cup (30 g) tapioca flour

3 cups (720 ml) Chicken Bone Broth (page 10)

¼ tsp turmeric

Sea salt to taste, we recommend Selina Naturally Celtic

Pepper, to taste

Fresh thyme, chopped, to taste

¼ cup (60 ml) heavy cream

Preheat the oven to 375°F (190°C). With a fork, stir together the almond flour, tapioca flour, salt and baking powder. Cut in the palm shortening until the mixture resembles coarse sand. Stir in cold water. Place in the refrigerator while you prepare the filling.

To make the filling, melt the butter in a large pot over medium-high heat, then add the onion, carrot and celery. Stir until the onions start to turn translucent, about 3 minutes. Stir in the chicken, sprinkle tapioca flour over the top and stir it until it's all combined. Cook for 1 minute, then pour in the chicken broth and stir well, letting it cook and thicken. Once it starts to thicken, add the turmeric, salt, pepper and thyme. Add the cream, then stir the mixture and let it bubble up and thicken, about 3 minutes. If it seems overly thick, splash in a little more broth. Turn off the heat. Pour the filling into a greased 2-quart (2-L) baking dish.

Check on your crust—it must be chilled completely! Take out the crust from the fridge and place it between 2 pieces of parchment paper. Use a rolling pin to roll it into a circle, then lay it on top of your baking dish. Place dish on a baking sheet and bake for 30 to 35 minutes or until the crust is golden brown. Cool for about 10 minutes before serving.

CHICKEN AND DUMPLINGS

Yes, you can make chicken and dumplings without using a packaged mix! This is a super-easy meal
to make during the week because you can get a precooked organic rotisserie chicken at the store.
Using real bone broth makes this dish extra creamy because of the gelatin in the broth.
Don't be surprised if you find yourself licking the bowl.

SERVES 6

BROTH

1 yellow onion, peeled and diced

5 stalks celery, diced

6 cups (1.5 L) Chicken Bone Broth
(page 10)

2 tsp (10 g) sea salt, we recommend
Selina Naturally Celtic

½ tsp ground sage

½ tsp ground thyme

½ tsp ground marjoram

½ tsp ground rosemary

½ tsp finely ground black pepper

3 cups (375 g) shredded rotisserie
chicken

¾ cup (115 g) green peas

½ cup (120 ml) raw milk

2 tbsp (15 g) tapioca flour

DUMPLINGS

1½ cups (165 g) blanched almonds,
slivered

½ cup (60 g) tapioca flour

½ tsp salt

⅓ cup (80 ml) chicken bone broth

2 tbsp (5 g) parsley, chopped

Place the onion, celery, broth, all seasonings besides parsley and salt in a soup
pot. Cover and let cook over medium heat for 15 to 20 minutes or until the
vegetables are soft. Add the shredded chicken and peas to the broth and simmer
for 10 minutes. In a small cup, combine the raw milk and tapioca flour; whisk well
and add this to the broth mixture. Continue to simmer on low heat.

Grind the slivered almonds into a fine flour in your blender or food processor. If
the almonds are not blending into a fine flour, add in ½ teaspoon of tapioca flour
and pulse. Add the tapioca flour and salt to the blender and pulse for 30 seconds.
Add broth and mix until you have soft dough. Roll the dough into 1-inch (2.5-cm)
balls to make about 10 to 12 dumplings. Drop the balls carefully into the soup and
cook for 15 minutes over medium-low heat. Add the parsley and serve.

See photo on page 102.

BEEF BOLOGNESE

We used to serve this dish in our restaurant and it was one of our biggest sellers. The cream makes the sauce incredibly rich. If you serve this with zoodles, make sure you slice them very thin. The sauce will hide the zoodles and your children will think it is pasta. I like to use spaghetti squash or kelp noodles. This dish can be easily packed for kids' lunches as well.

SERVES 4 TO 6

2 large carrots chopped into 1-inch (2.5-cm) pieces

2 celery stalks chopped into 1-inch (2.5-cm) pieces

2 cloves garlic

½ yellow onion, chopped

2 tbsp (30 ml) extra-virgin olive oil

Salt and pepper to taste

½ lb (225 g) grass-fed ground beef

1 lb (450 g) mild Italian sausage

½ cup (115 g) tomato paste

2 cups (475 ml) red wine, divided

2 bay leaves

Pinch of crushed red pepper flakes (optional)

3 cups (720 ml) Chicken or Beef Bone Broth (page 10 or 11), divided

¼ cup (60 ml) cream or half and half

Pasta of your choice or zoodles

Parmesan cheese, for garnishing

Fresh basil, for garnishing

Purée the carrots, celery, garlic and onion in a food processor until you have a thick paste. In a large saucepan, heat the olive oil over medium heat. Add puréed vegetables, salt and pepper. Sauté until cooked and light brown in color, about 10 minutes. Add the ground beef and Italian sausage, break it apart with a spoon and cook until the meat is browned. Add the tomato paste and stir with the other ingredients until it's well incorporated; cook for 2 minutes. Add ½ cup (120 ml) of red wine to deglaze the pan and break up any clumps of meat, then add the bay leaves, red pepper flakes, if using, and remaining wine and bring to a simmer. Cook until the wine is reduced by half, about 15 to 20 minutes. Add 1 cup (240 ml) of the broth, bring back to simmer and cook until reduced by two-thirds, about 30 minutes. Repeat, adding 1 cup (240 ml) of broth at a time, stirring well and simmering 30 minutes each time. Add the cream, and simmer on low while you cook your pasta. Cook the pasta and drain, reserving ½ cup (120 ml) of the pasta water. Add it to the sauce and if needed, add a little pasta water. Mix until the pasta is completely coated. Garnish with Parmesan and basil.

SPAGHETTI SQUASH CARBONARA AND PANCETTA

This was also one of our signature dishes in our restaurant. It's almost like breakfast for dinner with the eggs, ham and cream in the recipe. It's very heavy so it works perfectly with Paleo pasta.

SERVES 4

---

1 large spaghetti squash (about 2 lb [900 g])

1 tbsp (15 ml) extra-virgin olive oil

1 cup (225 g) diced pancetta

2 tsp (6 g) garlic, minced

¼ cup (59 ml) Chicken Bone Broth (page 10)

¾ cup (115 g) frozen peas

3 pastured organic large egg yolks

1 cup (180 g) Parmesan cheese, freshly grated

¼ cup (59 ml) heavy cream, preferably raw

2 tsp (10 g) sea salt, we recommend Selina Naturally Celtic

1¼ tsp (2.5 g) freshly cracked black pepper

Preheat the oven to 375°F (190°C). Poke the squash all over with a fork. Roast on a foil-lined pan for 1 to 1½ hours. Remove from the oven and set aside to cool. Once cooled, slice lengthwise and remove the seeds. Using a fork, shred the flesh of the spaghetti squash so that it resembles noodles. Transfer to a large bowl. In a large sauté pan over medium heat, add the olive oil and pancetta and cook until pancetta becomes crispy. Add the garlic and sauté for 1 minute. Add the broth and peas and cook until the liquid has completely evaporated. In a medium bowl, whisk the eggs, Parmesan and heavy cream, and then season with salt and pepper. Add the spaghetti squash to the pan with pancetta to reheat, tossing to combine. Pour the egg mixture over the spaghetti squash and mix well for 20 to 30 seconds, making sure not to cook the egg. Remove from the heat and continue to season to taste. Serve immediately.

DELICIOUS
MAIN DISHES

Including bone broth in your meals is a perfect way to ensure you are getting the nutrients you need. Adding it to your main dishes is a great habit to get into on your health journey. Hippocrates, the father of medicine, suggested we allow our food to be our medicine. I always encourage my clients to rotate, rotate, rotate their food choices. This includes the proteins you choose. Have beef one night, pork the next, then fish, then chicken, then do a night with just vegetables. When you walk into the produce section of the grocery store, you will find a variety of vegetables. Gorgeous red, yellow, green and purple vegetables. Rotating them will ensure you are supplying your body with a variety of minerals, vitamins and nutrients. Rotating your foods ensures you are getting all of the nutrition you can from your food. Don't get stuck in a rut and eat the same foods all the time. This is not a nourishing way to health. Plug bone broth into every recipe, starting with your daily main meals.

BRAISED SHORT RIBS OVER CAULIFLOWER GOAT CHEESE GOUDA GRITS

It would be difficult to choose my favorite recipe in this cookbook, but this one is in the top five for sure!
The cauliflower grits are so flavorful with the goat cheese Gouda added, they literally melt in your mouth.
I typically do not eat corn grits; however, this is when I cheat, and it is so worth it!
Need to impress someone? This is the meal to do it with.

SERVES 4

Kosher salt and pepper to taste

8 whole beef short ribs

1 large head of cauliflower, cut into florets

¼ cup (60 ml) bone broth

1 tbsp (15 g) ghee or butter

4 garlic cloves, minced

½ cup (30 g) goat cheese Gouda, shredded

Salt and pepper, to taste

2 tbsp (30 ml) extra-virgin olive oil

1 medium onion, diced

3 carrots, diced

2 shallots, peeled and finely minced

2 cups (480 ml) red or white wine

2 cups (480 ml) Beef Bone Broth (page 11)

1 tsp kosher salt

Freshly ground black pepper, to taste

2 sprigs thyme

2 sprigs rosemary

Salt and pepper the ribs and set aside.

Preheat the oven to 350°F (180°C). Place a couple inches of water in a large pot. Once the water is boiling, place a steamer insert and then cauliflower florets into the pot and cover. Steam for 12 to 14 minutes until completely tender. Drain and return the cauliflower to the pot. Add the broth, ghee and garlic to the cauliflower. Using an immersion blender, combine the ingredients. Once combined, stir in the cheese over low to medium heat until completely melted and combined. The cauliflower should be fairly thick and resemble the consistency of grits. Season with salt and pepper to taste and set aside.

Add the olive oil to a pan and raise the heat to high. Brown the ribs on all sides, about 45 seconds per side. Remove the ribs and set aside. Turn the heat to medium. Add the onion, carrots and shallots to the pan and cook for 2 minutes. Pour in the wine and scrape the bottom of the pan to release all the flavorful bits of glory. Bring to a boil and cook for 2 minutes. Add the broth, salt and pepper. Add more salt to taste. Add the ribs to the liquid; they should be almost completely submerged. Add the thyme and rosemary sprigs (whole) to the liquid. Put on the lid and place it into the oven. Cook at 350°F (180°C) for 2 hours, then reduce the heat to 325°F (160°C) and cook for an additional 30 to 45 minutes. The ribs should be fork-tender and falling off the bone. Remove the pan from the oven and allow the ribs to sit for at least 20 minutes, lid on. Heat up the grits, top with the short ribs and serve.

CRISPY CHICKEN AND CAULIFLOWER RISOTTO

When you make crispy chicken the right way, the juice of the chicken should spill onto your plate. I love how the juice of the chicken adds extra flavor to the risotto in this dish. Couple the flavorful chicken along with the cashew sage butter and this dish is explosive in flavor. The mascarpone in this recipe adds a very subtle cheese flavor and will make the dish extra creamy. Substituting bone broth for the water in the risotto adds extra protein and easily digested minerals to the dish. Remember to presoak all grains and rice to break down the phytic acid (see page 7 for soaking instructions).

SERVES 4

---

1 lb (450 g) cauliflower trimmed and roughly chopped

¾ stick (85 g) unsalted butter, divided

1 small brown onion, finely chopped

2 cloves garlic, crushed

⅔ cup (78 ml) dry white wine

1½ cups (340 g) arborio rice

6½ cups (1.5 L) warm Chicken Bone Broth (page 10), divided

2 tbsp (30 ml) extra-virgin olive oil

4 chicken breast fillets, skin on, wing bone in

Sea salt, we recommend Selina Naturally Celtic

Cracked black pepper, to taste

½ cup (75 g) cashews

5 to10 sage leaves

Mascarpone cheese, to serve

Place the cauliflower in a food processor and use short pulses until the mixture is finely chopped. Melt half the butter in a large frying pan over medium heat. Add the onion and garlic and cook, stirring for 5 minutes or until softened. Add the wine and cook for 2 minutes. Add the rice and cook, stirring, for 1 to 2 minutes. Cook, stirring frequently for 18 minutes while adding the broth 1 cup (240 ml) at a time, allowing it to absorb between each addition. Add the cauliflower and cook for another 5 to 7 minutes. While the risotto is cooking, heat the oil in a large nonstick frying pan over high heat. Add the chicken skin side down, sprinkle it with salt and pepper, cook for 3 to 4 minutes or until the skin is crisp, and then turn. Cover with a tight-fitting lid and cook for another 4 to 5 minutes or until just cooked through. Remove the chicken from the pan, cover loosely with aluminum foil and set aside. Wipe out the pan and return to medium heat. Add the cashews, sage and remaining butter, and cook for 2 to 3 minutes or until browned. Divide the risotto between plates and top with the mascarpone and cashew sage butter. Serve with the chicken.

SLOW-COOKED BEEF RAGU "PASTA"

This is another recipe from our restaurant days. This dish typically is found in the Northern Italian regions. Ragu is simply a sauce of meat and vegetables mixed together. This is the perfect dish to try spaghetti squash as your pasta alternative. Hide it well under the ragu and your children will never know.

SERVES 4 TO 6

2 lb (900 g) beef brisket, cut into 4 pieces

2 tbsp (30 g) arrowroot, for dusting

2 tbsp (30 g) ghee, coconut oil or bacon fat

¼ cup (60 ml) avocado oil

1 brown onion, thickly sliced

3 cloves of garlic, peeled and minced

1 cup (240 ml) dry red wine

2 cups (480 ml) Beef Bone Broth (page 11)

1 cup (240 ml) water

1 basket cherry tomatoes

4 bay leaves

½ cup (20 g) fresh basil leaves, chopped

2 tbsp (35 g) tomato paste

1 tbsp (15 g) coconut sugar

1 large spaghetti squash, cooked and shredded into spaghetti

Grated Parmesan

Preheat the oven to 350°F (180°C). Dust the beef with the arrowroot and shake to remove any excess. Heat the ghee in a heavy Dutch oven pan over medium heat. Cook the beef for 3 minutes on each side or until browned. Remove from the pan and set aside. Reduce the heat to low, add the avocado oil, onion and garlic and cook for 8 minutes or until softened. Increase the heat to high. Add the dry red wine and cook for 2 to 3 minutes or until the liquid is reduced by half. Add the beef bone broth, water, tomatoes, bay leaves, basil, tomato paste and coconut sugar and stir. Return the beef to the pan, cover and transfer to the oven to roast for 2 hours. Remove the lid and roast for 30 minutes more. Remove the beef from the pan and shred the meat using a fork. Return the meat to the sauce and mix to combine. Place on top of or toss with cooked, shredded spaghetti squash. Serve with grated cheese.

BONE BROTH PAELLA

The word *paella* comes from the Latin word for shallow pan, which is the type of pan used
to make this dish. Paella was introduced in Spain and was originally touted as a farmer's food. It was
a hearty meal for farmers and is a great post-workout meal. For those of you who are doing the
6-week clearing program, which is outlined at the end of the cookbook, this is a great
first dish back into rice and grains if you find that you can tolerate them.

SERVES 4

6 cloves garlic, peeled

1 onion, chopped

1 red or green bell pepper, seeded and chopped

10 threads of saffron

1 tbsp (3 g) thyme

2 tsp (5 g) sweet paprika

2 tsp (5 g) smoked paprika

1 small can crushed tomatoes

Sea salt and cracked pepper

½ tbsp (7 ml) extra-virgin olive oil

1 cup (230 g) dried chorizo, sliced

3 boneless chicken thighs, chopped

1½ cups (340 g) arborio rice or cauliflower rice

¼ cup (60 ml) sherry vinegar

2½ cups (600 ml) Chicken Bone Broth (page 10)

2 lb (900 g) mussels, cleaned

2 lb (900 g) raw shrimp or prawns, peeled and deveined

½ cup (75 g) frozen peas, thawed

Flat-leaf parsley leaves, for garnish

Place the garlic, onion, bell pepper, saffron, thyme, sweet and smoked paprika, tomatoes, salt and pepper in food processor and blend until smooth. Set aside.

Heat the oil in a large skillet. Add the chorizo and cook for 2 minutes. Add the chicken and cook for 3 more minutes or until browned. Add the rice and cook, stirring for 1 minute. Add the vinegar and cook for 1 minute. Add in the tomato sauce and chicken bone broth and bring to a boil. Push the mussels and the prawns into the rice and reduce the heat to low. Cook for 15 minutes without stirring. Increase the heat and cook for another 3 minutes. Remove the paella from the heat, top with the peas, cover with aluminum foil and set aside for 15 minutes or until most of the liquid is absorbed. Top with parsley before serving.

CRAB FRIED RICE

This is a great recipe for midweek quick meals. The crab adds a twist on this classic dish and the bone broth adds the flavor that fried rice can often lack unless you add loads of coconut aminos.

SERVES 4

3 cups (670 g) organic white rice

4 cups (960 ml) Chicken Bone Broth (page 10)

¼ cup (60 ml) coconut aminos

1½ tbsp (25 ml) rice vinegar

1 tsp sesame oil

Pinch of freshly ground white pepper

2 tbsp (30 ml) peanut oil

1 tbsp (5 g) fresh ginger, minced

3 garlic cloves, minced

3 green onions, thinly diced

2 large organic eggs, beaten

½ lb (250 g) fresh lump crabmeat

1 cup (150 g) frozen petite peas

In a saucepan on medium heat, add the rice and pour in the broth. Bring to a boil and cook until the surface bubbles. Reduce the heat to low; cover and cook for about 10 minutes, until the broth is gone. Let it stand for a few minutes before removing the lid. Remove the lid and fluff. In a small bowl, combine the coconut aminos, vinegar, sesame oil and white pepper and stir. Heat a wok or large nonstick fry pan over high heat until very hot and pour in the peanut oil. Add the ginger, garlic and green onions and stir-fry until fragrant, about 5 seconds. Add the rice and stir-fry until the rice is hot, about 5 minutes. Create a small well in the middle of the rice that reaches the bottom of the pan. Add the eggs to the well and immediately stir-fry to incorporate them into the rice. Once the eggs are cooked through, add the crabmeat, peas and sauce and stir-fry until well combined and heated through, 2 to 3 minutes.

OLIVE, RICOTTA AND POLENTA BAKE

We have this categorized under a meal, but you could certainly use this as
a side dish for a dinner party. It is so easy to make.

SERVES 4

1½ cups (360 ml) Chicken Bone Broth (page 10)

1½ tbsp (20 g) unsalted butter

Sea salt, we recommend Selina Naturally Celtic

Cracked pepper, to taste

½ cup (85 g) organic polenta, we recommend Bob's Red Mill

½ cup (90 g) Parmesan, finely grated

½ cup (115 g) ricotta

½ cup (125 g) cherry tomatoes

⅔ cup (25 g) pitted black olives

⅔ cup (25 g) pitted kalamata olives

½ cup (50 g) baby arugula leaves

Place the broth, butter, salt and pepper in a frying pan over medium heat. Bring to a boil and gradually stir in the polenta. Cook, stirring for 1 minute or until thickened. Top with the Parmesan, ricotta, tomatoes and olives and place under the broiler for 10 to 12 minutes or until golden. Top with arugula and serve.

ADOBO SHRIMP WITH BONE BROTH SPANISH RICE

Adding bone broth to any rice dish adds so many flavors to the rice that you often don't need to add any other spices or herbs. Additionally, substituting bone broth for the liquid in the rice adds protein, gelatin and minerals! This is a great dish to serve on its own or as a side to another protein while having a summer BBQ.

SERVES 4

1 small can chipotle chilies in adobo sauce

1 tbsp (15 ml) freshly squeezed lime juice

1 tbsp (15 ml) extra-virgin olive oil

½ tbsp (5 g) cumin

Sea salt to taste, we recommend Selina Naturally Celtic

Freshly ground pepper, to taste

1 lb (450 g) wild-caught, medium-size shrimp, peeled and deveined

2 tbsp (30 ml) extra-virgin olive oil, divided

1 medium white onion, minced

1 medium green bell pepper, de-seeded and chopped

1 clove garlic, minced

1 jalapeño, de-seeded and minced (optional)

2 cups (480 ml) Chicken Bone Broth (page 10)

6 oz (170 g) organic tomato paste

1 cup (210 g) organic basmati rice

Fresh lime wedges, for garnish

Combine 1 tablespoon (15 ml) of the adobo sauce, 1 chili out of the can, lime juice, olive oil, cumin, salt and pepper in a large plastic bag and add the shrimp. Shake well and place in the fridge to marinate for 30 minutes. After marinating, heat 1 tablespoon (15 ml) olive oil in a frying pan over medium heat and add the shrimp to sauté. Cook until the pink flesh becomes white, flipping frequently to prevent overcooking.

While the shrimp is marinating, heat the remaining 1 tablespoon (15 ml) of olive oil and sauté the onion, bell pepper, garlic and jalapeño, if using, in a medium pot until slightly softened. Add the bone broth and tomato paste. Bring to a boil. Stir in the salt and rice, reduce the heat and cook until tender, about 20 minutes. Salt to taste. Serve the shrimp over rice and garnish with fresh lime wedges.

SAUTÉED CHICKEN
WITH PEACH-BALSAMIC GLAZE

This is a recipe that was passed back and forth among my clients. The peach jam and balsamic vinegar pair well together. If you do the 6-week clearing program that I outline at the end of the book, and you finally kick your sugar habit, you will find that you can really taste the sweetness of the jam in this recipe.

SERVES 4

2 tbsp (30 g) butter

2 cloves garlic, sliced

1 lb (450 g) chicken breasts or thighs

¼ cup (60 ml) dry sherry or white wine

¼ cup (60 ml) Chicken Bone Broth (page 10)

2 tsp (2 g) chopped fresh tarragon

¼ cup (60 ml) organic peach jam

1 tsp balsamic vinegar or to taste

Melt the butter with the garlic in a large skillet over low heat. Allow it to bubble slowly for about 10 minutes to infuse the garlic into the butter, then remove the garlic and reserve. Increase the heat to medium-high. When hot, cook the chicken until golden brown on both sides, about 3 minutes per side, then set aside. Pour the sherry into the skillet and allow it to simmer for 20 seconds. Stir in the chicken bone broth, tarragon and jam. Bring back to a simmer, then reduce the heat to medium-low, cover and simmer for 5 minutes. Add the vinegar, and cook covered for 2 minutes. Return the chicken to the pan and simmer until fully cooked, 3 to 5 minutes.

MONGOLIAN BEEF

Children can be picky eaters, rejecting food simply because of its texture or shape.
My clients often complain that they can't get their children to eat nourishing foods. Getting creative
with the shape or cut of the meat is key. This is a dish that you can experiment with. Cut the beef
into tiny squares and give to your picky eater. Add extra sea salt to the meat when presenting it
to your children and you may find that they suddenly love beef. I also love to introduce cauliflower
fried rice instead of white rice under this dish to children. They can't tell the difference.

SERVES 4

---

2 tsp (10 ml) coconut oil, plus ½ cup (120 ml) coconut oil for frying, more if needed

1 tbsp (5 g) fresh ginger, minced

3 garlic cloves, chopped

½ cup (120 ml) coconut aminos

½ cup (120 ml) Beef Bone Broth (page 11)

½ cup (120 ml) honey

1 lb (450 g) flank steak

¼ cup (40 g) tapioca flour

2 large green onions, plus more for garnish, sliced on the diagonal into 1-inch (2.5-cm) lengths

Heat 2 teaspoons (30 ml) coconut oil in a medium saucepan over medium heat. Don't let the oil get too hot. Add the ginger and garlic to the pan and quickly add the coconut aminos and broth before the garlic scorches. Add the honey to the sauce, stirring well, then boil the sauce for 2 to 3 minutes or until the sauce thickens. Remove from the heat. Slice the flank steak against the grain into ¼-inch (6-mm) bite-size slices. Dip the steak pieces into the tapioca flour to apply a very thin dusting to both sides of each piece of beef. Let the beef sit for about 10 minutes so the tapioca flour sticks. As the beef sits, heat up at least ½ cup (120 ml) coconut oil in a wok or skillet over medium heat until it's nice and hot, but not smoking. Add the beef to the oil and sauté for just 2 minutes or until the beef just begins to darken around the edges. Stir the meat around a little so that it cooks evenly. After a couple minutes, use a large slotted spoon to remove meat and place onto paper towels, then pour the oil out of the wok or skillet. Put the pan back over the heat, return the meat back into it and simmer for 1 minute. Add the sauce, cook for 1 minute while stirring, then add all the green onions. Cook for 1 more minute, then remove the beef and onions with tongs or a slotted spoon to a serving plate. Spoon the sauce over the beef and garnish with green onions.

WHITE WINE CHICKEN AND CITRUS POTATOES

This is a great meal to serve in the summertime. The zest in the citrus potatoes is calmed by the addition of the bone broth. If you don't like artichokes you can leave them out. Remember the trick to introducing new foods to children is to cut them into tiny, tiny pieces and serve with plenty of sea salt. You can try it with the artichokes in this dish.

SERVES 4

---

1 tbsp (15 ml) extra-virgin olive oil

2 lb (900 g) chicken breast or thighs

Sea salt to taste, we recommend Selina Naturally Celtic

Cracked black pepper, to taste

4 marinated artichokes, halved

2 cloves garlic, thinly sliced

1 lb (450 g) organic soaked baby potatoes, cut into ½-inch (1.3-cm) slices

1 cup (240 ml) Chicken Bone Broth (page 10)

½ cup (120 ml) dry white wine

8 sprigs thyme

2 tbsp (30 ml) lemon juice

Pecorino (sheep's milk), finely grated for garnish

Heat the oil in an ovenproof saucepan over high heat. Sprinkle the chicken with salt and pepper and cook for 2 to 3 minutes on each side or until browned. Remove from the pan and set aside. Add artichokes and cook for 1 to 2 minutes on each side. Add the garlic and cook for 30 seconds or until lightly browned. Add the potatoes, broth, wine and thyme and bring to a boil. Top with the chicken, cover with a tight-fitting lid and reduce the heat to medium. Cook for 10 to 12 minutes or until the chicken is cooked through and the potatoes are tender. Add the lemon juice and stir to combine. Top with the pecorino and pepper to serve.

CHICKEN MOLE

Mole is a generic term used for a variety of sauces in Mexican cuisine. Oftentimes chocolate is added to the sauce to counteract the spice of the pepper. Don't be afraid to cook with chocolate. It is very easy and adds depth and flavor to the sauce.

SERVES 4

2 tbsp (30 g) lard or tallow

3 garlic cloves, pressed

1 yellow onion, roughly chopped

2 tbsp (15 g) chili powder

½ tbsp (5 g) cayenne pepper

1 tsp ground cumin

2 tsp (5 g) cinnamon

1 (14.5-oz [600-ml]) can organic diced tomatoes, drained

2 or 3 chipotle peppers, chopped

3 tbsp (20 g) unsweetened cocoa powder

3 tbsp (50 g) almond butter

¼ cup (60 ml) Chicken Bone Broth (page 10), plus 1 tbsp (15 ml)

1 lb (450 g) organic chicken thighs and breasts

1 tbsp (15 g) coconut oil

½ yellow cabbage, roughly chopped

½ purple cabbage, roughly chopped

Sea salt to taste, we recommend Selina Naturally Celtic

Black pepper, to taste

Heat the fat in a large sauté pan over medium heat. Add the garlic and stir. Add the onion and cook until it's translucent. Add spices and continue to cook. Add the diced tomatoes, chipotle peppers, cocoa powder and almond butter and mix together well. The mixture will be thick. Once it's well combined, add the broth in small amounts until you get the preferred consistency. Add the chicken to the pan and mix with the sauce until the chicken is coated. Cover and let cook for about 20 to 25 minutes, depending on how thick your pieces of chicken are. While the chicken is cooking, heat the coconut oil in another sauté pan. Add the chopped cabbage to the pan, add the remaining broth, stir, cover and let cook for about 15 minutes, stirring occasionally to prevent the cabbage from burning. Add salt and pepper to taste. To serve, spoon the sauce over the chicken in small bowls and top with cabbage.

GINGER-AND-HONEY-GLAZED CHICKEN THIGHS WITH BABY BOK CHOY

The ginger, lime and honey in this recipe make for the perfect burst of flavor. This is a meal that I pack cold for lunch for both my husband and my children. Don't leave out the fish sauce. (Red Boat is my favorite brand.) You could also use chicken breast, but the thighs are a bit more tender.

SERVES 4

½ cup (120 ml) local, organic honey

2 tbsp (30 ml) coconut aminos or gluten-free tamari sauce

2 tsp (10 ml) fish sauce

2 tbsp (30 ml) lime juice

1 tbsp (5 g) fresh ginger, peeled and finely grated

2 cloves garlic, crushed

½ cup (120 ml) Chicken Bone Broth (page 10)

2 tbsp (30 ml) sesame oil

1½ lb (750 g) boneless skinless chicken thighs, trimmed and cut into cubes

1 lime, thinly sliced

Fresh baby bok choy, steamed or lightly sautéed in olive oil

Shredded green onion

Place the honey, aminos, fish sauce, lime juice, ginger, garlic and bone broth in a bowl and mix to combine; set aside. Heat the oil in a wok over high heat, add the chicken and cook in batches for 6 minutes or until cooked through. Add the honey mixture and lime, bring to a boil and cook for 4 to 6 minutes or until slightly thickened. Arrange the bok choy greens onto a plate and top with the chicken and green onion.

SEARED HALIBUT IN CHORIZO AND TOMATO BONE BROTH

Chorizo and fish? Yes, please! When I was young, my mom would often make chorizo and eggs for breakfast. Back then, there weren't many healthy options, but today you can find many healthy versions of chorizo in stores. You can even use a turkey version. Just make sure you look at the ingredients to rule out the use of MSG or unidentified flavorings, which can mean MSG.

SERVES 4

2½ tbsp (35 ml) extra-virgin olive oil, divided

½ small onion, minced

3 medium cloves garlic, halved and thinly sliced

¼ cup (60 g) finely diced Spanish chorizo

½ cup (120 ml) dry white wine

⅔ cup (155 ml) Chicken Bone Broth (page 10)

1½ tsp (7.5 ml) sherry vinegar

1 (14.5-oz [600-ml]) can organic crushed tomatoes

2½ tsp (5 g) pimentón smoked paprika, divided

⅔ tsp crushed red pepper flakes

2 sprigs thyme

Sea salt to taste, we recommend Selina Naturally Celtic

Black pepper, to taste

4 wild-caught halibut fillets

¼ cup (5 g) flat-leaf parsley, roughly chopped

Heat 1 tablespoon (15 ml) olive oil in a medium saucepan over medium heat until shimmering. Add the onion and garlic and cook, stirring, until slightly softened, about 3 minutes. Add the chorizo and continue to cook until the sausage is lightly browned, about 4 minutes. Add wine and increase the heat to medium-high. Bring to a boil and simmer until reduced by half, about 1 minute. Add the chicken broth, vinegar, tomatoes, 1½ teaspoons (3 g) paprika, red pepper and thyme. Reduce the heat and simmer for 20 minutes, stirring occasionally. Season to taste with salt and pepper.

While the sauce is simmering, season the fish with salt, pepper and paprika. Heat the remaining 1½ tablespoons (22 ml) olive oil in a large skillet over high heat until shimmering. Carefully place the halibut in the pan skin side down. Cook without moving until the skin is crisp and nicely browned, about 3 minutes. Carefully flip the fish, reduce the heat to medium and continue cooking until the fish is firm to the touch and no longer opaque, 4 to 5 minutes. Spoon the cooking liquid from the pan over the fish to prevent it from drying out. Transfer the fish to a paper towel–lined plate to rest. Serve the halibut in a bowl and ladle a generous amount of chorizo broth over the top. Garnish with parsley and serve.

BLUE CHEESE—CRUSTED FILET MIGNON WITH PORT WINE SAUCE

Bone broth is rich in amino acids that do everything from assist with leaky gut syndrome to help athletes recover more quickly after workouts. Sneaking it into every meal ensures vital nutrients and minerals for your body. The bone broth adds depth to this port wine sauce.

SERVES 4

1 tbsp (15 g) butter or ghee

½ cup (80 g) white onion, minced

3 cloves garlic, minced

1 tbsp (5 g) fresh thyme, chopped

¾ cup (180 ml) Beef Bone Broth (page 11)

½ cup (120 ml) port wine

1 tbsp (15 ml) extra-virgin olive oil

4 grass-fed filet mignon steaks

¾ cup (100 g) crumbled raw blue cheese

Melt the butter in a skillet over medium heat. Add the onion, garlic and thyme. Cook, stirring constantly until the onion is tender. Stir in the beef broth, scraping any onion bits from the bottom of the pan, then stir in the port wine. Bring to a boil, and cook until the mixture has reduced to about a ½ cup (120 ml). Set aside. This may also be made ahead of time and reheated.

Preheat the oven to 350°F (175°C). Heat the oil in a cast-iron or other oven-safe skillet over high heat. Sear the steaks quickly on both sides until brown, then place the whole pan into the oven. Roast the steaks in the oven for about 15 minutes for medium rare, with an internal temperature of 145°F (63°C). You may adjust this time to allow the steaks to finish just below your desired degree of doneness if medium rare is not what you prefer. Remove from the oven, and place on a baking sheet. Top each steak with a layer of blue cheese. Preheat the broiler. Place the steaks under the preheated broiler until the cheese topping is browned and bubbly, about 3 to 4 minutes. Remove from broiler, and let stand for at least 15 minutes before serving. Serve with warm port wine sauce.

LEMON POACHED SALMON

Looking for ways to sneak broth into your children's meals? This is a great one. Most children will eat salmon (if trained from an early age), but getting them to drink their broth can be a whole different challenge. Adding broth to this simple recipe adds the extra nutrients to the dish and the poached salmon hides the broth.

SERVES 4

---

1 large lemon, juiced

⅓ cup (80 ml) Chicken Bone Broth (page 10)

2 salmon fillets

2 pats grass-fed, organic butter

½ lemon, thinly sliced

Place the lemon juice and broth in a medium saucepan. Add salmon fillets. Top each fillet with one pat of butter. Bring the liquid to slow boil over medium-low heat. Reduce the heat slightly, cover and simmer for 5 minutes. Flip the salmon over, cover and continue to simmer for 5 more minutes or until the salmon is cooked through. Remove the salmon and spoon the broth sauce over each fillet. Top with sliced lemon and serve.

BBQ PULLED PORK WITH HOMEMADE BARBECUE SAUCE

My clients often forget that sauces can be healthy. This barbecue sauce is not only flavorful, but it is nutritious. Make extra and freeze it to use in other recipes such as hamburgers or ribs. Bottled sauces are sources of what I refer to as the bloat. You can prepare perfectly healthful food then load on dressings, sauces and unhealthy oils and end up bloated and feeling 5 pounds (2 kg) heavier just because of the sauce you added.

SERVES 4

---

2 cups (480 ml) Beef Bone Broth (page 11)

3 lb (1.5 kg) boneless pork ribs

HOMEMADE BARBECUE SAUCE

1 medium onion, chopped

2 garlic cloves, minced

2 tbsp (30 ml) organic, extra-virgin olive oil

1 tbsp (7.5 g) chili powder

2 tbsp (30 ml) organic Worcestershire sauce

2 tbsp (30 ml) mustard

⅓ cup (80 ml) honey

1 cup (240 ml) organic tomato sauce

1 tsp seasoning salt

2 tbsp (30 ml) apple cider vinegar

Pepper, to taste

Pour the beef broth into a slow cooker and add the boneless pork ribs. Cook on high heat for 4 hours or until the meat shreds easily. Remove the meat and shred with two forks.

To make the barbecue sauce, cook the onion and garlic in oil until tender. Add the remaining ingredients and bring to a boil. Reduce to a simmer and cook uncovered for 30 minutes, stirring occasionally. Remove from the heat and set aside. Preheat the oven to 350°F (177°C). Transfer the shredded pork to a Dutch oven or iron skillet and stir in 2 cups (480 ml) of the homemade barbecue sauce. Bake for 30 minutes.

SHERRY AND WILD MUSHROOM CHICKEN

The sherry in this dish adds a warm smoky flavor to the chicken. If you don't have sherry on hand you can substitute it by combining ½ cup (120 ml) apple cider vinegar and ½ cup water (120 ml) with 2 tablespoons (30 g) coconut sugar and 1 teaspoon lemon juice for 1 cup (240 ml) of sherry wine.

SERVES 4 TO 6

2 lb (900 g) organic, pastured, skinless, boneless chicken thighs

Sea salt, we recommend Selina Naturally Celtic

Freshly ground black pepper

½ cup (120 ml) olive oil

½ shallot, minced

8 whole garlic cloves, plus 3 cloves, minced

1½ lb (680 g) porcini and cremini mushroom blend, diced without stems

8 sprigs fresh thyme, tied with kitchen string

¼ cup (60 ml) dry sherry

2 cups (480 ml) white wine

2¼ cups (533 ml) Chicken Bone Broth (page 10), divided

2 tsp (5 g) arrowroot

3 tbsp (45 g) unsalted butter, at room temperature

Preheat the oven to 325°F (160°C). Pat the chicken dry with paper towels and sprinkle both sides liberally with salt and pepper. In a large Dutch oven, heat the oil and shallot. Add the chicken in three batches, leaving plenty of space between pieces, and brown lightly over medium-high heat for 3 to 5 minutes on each side. Transfer the chicken to a plate and continue until all the chicken is browned.

Add the whole garlic cloves, mushrooms and thyme to the pot, and cook over medium heat for 5 minutes, stirring occasionally. Add the sherry and cook for 1 minute, scraping up the brown bits. Add the minced garlic and cook for 2 more minutes. Add the wine, 2 cups (480 ml) broth, ½ tablespoon (9 g) salt and 1 teaspoon pepper and bring to a simmer. Add the chicken, cover and place in the middle of the oven for 30 to 35 minutes until the chicken is cooked through. Remove the pot from the oven, remove the chicken and set aside in a bowl. Whisk ¼ cup (60 ml) bone broth and the arrowroot together to make a slurry. Stir the slurry into the simmering sauce 1 tablespoon (15 ml) at a time, and heat for 1 minute or until thickened. Once thickened, add the butter. Add the chicken back into the pot, mix well and serve.

BONE BROTH OSSO BUCCO

My son Blake loves to try new foods. He ordered this dish at a restaurant, and I had to come up with a version that was similar because it was a big hit at our table that night. Make extra because it is hard to stop eating this once you start. The Osso Bucco is braised in the broth, which gives a deep richness to the dish.

SERVES 4 TO 6

1 cup (30 g) dried porcini mushrooms

2 cups (480 ml) hot water

Ghee, for sautéing

2 or 3 grass-fed beef shanks, about 2 inches (5 cm) thick

¾ cup (115 g) organic onion, chopped

2 tbsp (30 g) butter

1 cup (100 g) of organic celery, diced

1 cup (150 g) organic carrots, chopped

¼ cup (60 ml) red wine

2 cups (480 ml) Beef Bone Broth (page 11)

Sea salt to taste, we recommend Selina Naturally Celtic

Pepper, to taste

1 bay leaf

Put mushrooms in a small bowl with about 2 cups (480 ml) of filtered hot water and let sit until soft. In a large skillet melt the ghee and sauté the beef shanks on high heat until browned on all sides. In a cast-iron skillet add the onions and 2 tablespoons (30 g) of butter over medium-low heat. Stir them so that onions are coated; cover and leave them for 5 minutes. Uncover, stir in the celery and carrots and cover for 5 minutes more until the onions are soft and translucent. When the vegetables are softened, add the shanks, raise the heat and add the red wine. Sauté on high until all the wine has evaporated. Add the mushrooms and soaking liquid, broth, salt, pepper and bay leaf, and reduce the heat to low. Cover and let simmer for 2 hours, stirring occasionally. To serve, remove the shanks from the pot and liberally spoon the sauce over them.

CHICKEN SALTIMBOCCA

Traditional saltimbocca is made with veal and topped with prosciutto. My twist is with chicken. Make sure the prosciutto you purchase is cut paper-thin as it can become very chewy if it isn't thin enough for this recipe.

SERVES 6

6 organic chicken cutlets, flattened

Sea salt to taste, we recommend Selina Naturally Celtic

Freshly ground black pepper, to taste

6 paper-thin slices prosciutto

1½ cups (337 g) frozen spinach, thawed, excess water squeezed out and chopped

3 tbsp (45 ml) organic olive oil, divided

¼ cup (45 g) grated pecorino Romano

Toothpicks

1 cup (240 ml) Chicken Bone Broth (page 10)

2 tbsp (30 ml) fresh lemon juice

Thinly sliced lemon, for garnishing

Lay the chicken cutlets flat on a plate and sprinkle with salt and pepper. Lay 1 slice of prosciutto over each cutlet. In a bowl, season the drained spinach with salt and pepper and toss with 1 tablespoon (15 ml) oil, coating well. Arrange a thin layer of spinach over the prosciutto and chicken cutlets and sprinkle pecorino evenly over each cutlet. Carefully roll each cutlet into a roll and secure with a toothpick. In a large skillet over high heat, heat remaining 2 tablespoons (30 ml) of oil. Gently add the chicken rolls and cook for 2 minutes until golden brown on all sides. Add in the chicken broth and lemon juice, and use a wooden spoon to scrape the bottom of the pan to remove the browned bits. Bring the liquid to a boil. Reduce the heat to medium. Cover and simmer until the chicken is just cooked through, about 8 to 10 minutes. Remove the chicken to a serving plate with tongs and set aside. Continue to simmer the cooking liquid over high heat until it is reduced, about 5 minutes. To serve, remove the toothpicks from chicken rolls and drizzle the reduced sauce over them. Garnish with lemon slices.

BEEF STROGANOFF

Using arrowroot instead of an old-fashioned roux is a great way to thicken sauces. Arrowroot powder is derived from the South American plant *Maranta arundinacea*. Keep this on hand to thicken any recipe, even desserts. I use it in my beef stroganoff. The bone broth smooths out the chalkiness of the arrowroot powder, ensuring a rich, creamy sauce. This recipe also calls for Worcestershire sauce. Always buy organic Worcestershire sauce, as the regular one is loaded with MSG.

SERVES 4 TO 6

½ lb (225 g) grass-fed ground beef

½ lb (225 g) organic, pastured ground pork

1 large organic egg

¼ cup (25 g) almond flour

1 tsp kosher salt

¼ tsp black pepper, plus more

½ tsp garlic powder

½ tsp onion powder

1 tsp dried parsley

1 tsp paprika

1 tsp organic Worcestershire sauce

2 tbsp (30 g) butter or ghee

2 cups (130 g) cremini mushrooms, sliced

1 cup (130 g) yellow onions, sliced

1 clove garlic, minced

1½ cups (360 ml) Beef Bone Broth (page 11)

¾ cup (90 g) organic sour cream

¼ tsp arrowroot powder

Sea salt to taste, we recommend Selina Naturally Celtic

2 tbsp (5 g) fresh parsley, chopped

Preheat the oven to 425°F (220°C). Combine the meatball ingredients in a medium bowl and mix well. Form into 12 meatballs. Place the meatballs onto a foiled baking sheet and bake for 20 to 25 minutes.

While the meatballs are baking, place the butter and the mushrooms in a skillet. Cook until the mushrooms are golden and fragrant, about 4 to 5 minutes. Remove the mushrooms from the pan. Add the onions and garlic and cook for 3 to 4 minutes until the onions are soft and translucent. Remove the onions from the pan. Add the beef broth to the pan and scrape the bottom of the pan with a wooden spoon to remove brown bits (keep these in there, that's all the flavor!). Whisk in the sour cream and arrowroot powder until smooth. Add the mushrooms, onions and garlic back to the pan and stir. Season with salt and pepper to taste. Simmer on low for 20 minutes. Once the meatballs are cooked, remove them from the oven and set aside to rest for 5 minutes. Using tongs, place the meatballs into the stroganoff pan and stir gently to coat well. Let sit over low heat for 2 to 3 minutes, and then serve topped with fresh parsley.

ENCHILADAS VERDE WITH PICKLED RED ONION

The pickled red onion really makes this dish. Make extra so you get some in every bite.
Get your smartphone out—you will want to take a picture of this one to show all your friends
what a wonderful cook you are.

SERVES 4 TO 6

½ cup (120 ml) Bragg's apple cider vinegar

1 tbsp (15 g) coconut sugar

1½ tsp (7.5 g) sea salt

1 red onion, thinly sliced

3 tbsp (45 ml) extra-virgin olive oil

1 large onion, minced

5 or 6 cloves garlic, minced or pressed

1½ lb (750 g) tomatillos, husked and quartered

2 green peppers, chopped

1 or 2 jalapeños, seeded and membranes removed

½ bunch cilantro, coarsely chopped

4 cups (960 ml) Chicken Bone Broth (page 10)

1½ tsp (7.5 g) sea salt, we recommend Selina Naturally Celtic

¼ tsp black pepper

1½ tsp (3 g) cumin

Coconut oil, for greasing baking dish

1 package organic, sprouted corn tortillas or homemade Paleo tortillas

1 lb (450 g) shredded rotisserie chicken

10 oz (280 g) raw, shredded jack cheese

Cilantro, for garnishing

Lime wedge, for garnishing

To make the pickled red onion, whisk the first 3 ingredients and 1 cup (240 ml) water in a small bowl until the sugar and salt dissolve. Place the onion in a jar and pour the vinegar mixture over it. Let it sit at room temperature for 1 to 2 hours. Drain and set aside.

In a large saucepan or stockpot, heat the olive oil over medium heat. Sauté onion and garlic until tender. While the onion and garlic are cooking, combine the tomatillos, green peppers, jalapeño peppers and cilantro in a blender. Process until smooth. If the mixture is too thick, add broth ¼ cup (60 ml) at a time. Pour the tomatillo mixture over the onion and garlic and add the broth, salt, pepper and cumin. Simmer over medium heat for 30 minutes. Set sauce aside while making the enchiladas.

Preheat the oven to 350°F (180°C). Lightly grease a medium baking dish with coconut oil. Fill each tortilla with equal amounts of chicken and cheese, reserving ¼ cup (25 g) cheese for topping. Roll the tortillas to form enchiladas. Arrange enchiladas in the prepared baking dish. Cover with the sauce. Bake for 30 minutes. Top with the reserved cheese and continue baking for 5 minutes until cheese is melted. Serve garnished with the pickled red onion, cilantro and lime wedge.

MUSHROOM RAGU AND ZUCCHINI PAPPARDELLE

Variety is the key to health. Eating meat seven nights a week is not a good idea. Rotating chicken, meat, fish and having a nonmeat night is a great way to plan for a week's worth of meals. All of you Paleoites, one night of vegetables is okay. Although the protein in the bone broth is not a complete protein, it is fine to use in place of meat once in a while. It also gives your gallbladder a break from having to handle all of the fat in your meat.

SERVES 4

---

2 large zucchini

½ tsp salt

Coconut oil, for cooking

2½ tbsp (35 g) butter

1 clove garlic, crushed

2 tsp (3 g) thyme leaves

2 cups (250 g) mixed cremini and porcini mushrooms, halved

1¼ cups (300 ml) Beef Bone Broth (page 11)

Pecorino Romano, grated, for garnishing

Freshly cracked pepper, to taste

Trim off the ends of the zucchini. Make pappardelle-shaped pieces by using a vegetable peeler and slicing lengthwise. Your strips should be ¾- to 1-inch (2.0- to 2.5-cm) wide. Place the zucchini pappardelle in one layer across some paper towels. Sprinkle with salt on both sides and top with another layer of paper towels. Place a baking sheet over the paper towels and weigh it down with a skillet. This will help remove some dampness from the noodles. Let the zucchini sit for 20 to 30 minutes. Once weeped, gently add the zucchini pappardelle to a coconut-oiled nonstick pan and cook on low for 30 seconds on each side. Remove from the skillet, place in a bowl and cover well.

Heat a frying pan over high heat. Add the butter, garlic and thyme and cook for 30 seconds. Add the mushrooms and cook for 4 minutes or until well browned. Add the bone broth and simmer for 4 minutes or until the mushrooms are soft. Serve the zucchini pappardelle topped with the mushroom ragu. Garnish with pecorino and pepper.

MUSHROOM, SPINACH AND BACON RISOTTO BAKE

This dish is a little different from a traditional risotto because it is baked. The baking blends all the flavors together so nicely. Resist the urge to peek under the aluminum foil because you will lose the steam that cooks the rice.

SERVES 4

1 tbsp (15 ml) extra-virgin olive oil

1 clove garlic, crushed

¾ cup (95 g) cremini mushrooms, roughly chopped

4 slices bacon, roughly chopped

1 cup (230 g) organic arborio rice

2½ cups (600 ml) Chicken Bone Broth (page 10)

Handful of baby spinach leaves, stems removed

½ cup (90 g) pecorino Romano, finely grated

1½ tbsp (21 g) butter or ghee

Sea salt to taste, we recommend Selina Naturally Celtic

Cracked black pepper, to taste

Preheat the oven to 350°F (180°C). Heat the oil in a large nonstick frying pan over medium heat. Add the garlic, mushrooms and bacon, and cook for 5 minutes or until the bacon is cooked and browned. Place in a 5-cup (1.25-L) ovenproof dish with the rice and broth and stir to combine. Cover tightly with aluminum foil and bake for 40 minutes or until most of the broth is absorbed and the rice is al dente. Stir in the spinach, Romano and butter. Season with salt and pepper.

SPAGHETTI SQUASH PAD THAI

Once you start using spaghetti squash in place of pasta it will be hard to go back to pasta.
And why would you? Spaghetti squash is a great source of vitamin A and potassium. Make sure you
don't overcook the squash as it can become mushy. My son Clayton could live on noodles if it was healthy.
I add the bone broth to his noodle dishes or substitute with zoodles, which are noodles made
from zucchini, or spaghetti squash noodles to ensure he is well-nourished.

SERVES 4

1 large spaghetti squash

Salt and pepper to taste

½ tbsp (7 g) coconut oil

1 clove garlic, minced

1 cup (100 g) shredded green cabbage

1 cup (150 g) organic carrots, thinly sliced

¼ cup (60 ml) Chicken Bone Broth (page 10)

2 tbsp (30 g) organic sunflower or almond butter

1½ tbsp (22 ml) coconut aminos

1 tbsp (15 ml) rice wine vinegar

1 red chili pepper

2 cooked organic chicken breast or thighs, chopped

1 green onion, chopped

1 small bunch of cilantro, chopped

1 lime wedge

Preheat the oven to 350°F (180°C). Cut the spaghetti squash in half lengthwise and scrape away the seeds. Season with salt and pepper and place the cut sides down on a lined and covered cookie sheet. Roast for 50 to 60 minutes. To test if it is done, pierce the skin of the squash with a fork, and if it is pierced easily, remove it from the oven and set aside to cool. Once cooled, use a large fork to shred the spaghetti squash lengthwise to create noodle-length strips, and then set the squash noodles aside in a large bowl.

In a large nonstick skillet melt coconut oil and sauté the garlic for 1 minute. Add the cabbage and carrots and sauté over medium-high heat for 3 minutes. Transfer vegetables to a plate. Add the broth, nut butter, coconut aminos, rice vinegar and red chili pepper to the skillet. Whisk well and heat until smooth. Return the veggies and spaghetti squash to the pan. Add the chicken, stirring well, and heat over medium heat for 5 minutes or until the sauce has coated all the chicken. Garnish with green onion, cilantro and lime.

PRIMAVERA QUINOA WITH KALE PESTO

Kale is a really versatile vegetable. One way to incorporate it into your diet is by making a pesto out of it. I make extra pesto and add it to scrambled eggs and vegetables. You can freeze the pesto to have on hand when the in-laws pop in for the weekend and you want to impress them with a great breakfast.

SERVES 4 TO 6

3 cups (135 g) organic fresh basil

½ cups (65 g) pine nuts

3 bunches fresh kale, shredded

2 or 3 cloves garlic

⅓ cup (80 ml) cold-pressed organic olive oil

Sea salt to taste, we recommend Selina Naturally Celtic

Freshly ground pepper, to taste

1½ cups (250 g) quinoa, uncooked

1 lb (450 g) organic, boneless skinless chicken breasts

4 cups (960 ml) Chicken Bone Broth (page 10), divided

4 to 6 cloves garlic

Salt and pepper, to taste

1 tbsp (15 ml) extra-virgin olive oil

¾ cup (180 ml) kale pesto

2½ cups (450 g) organic frozen peas

1 squeeze lemon juice

Pecorino Romano, for serving

Put the basil, pine nuts, kale and garlic in a food processor and pulse until finely chopped. Drizzle in cold-pressed olive oil until the desired consistency is reached. Add salt and pepper to taste. Spoon into a container and set aside.

Rinse the quinoa. Place the quinoa, chicken, 3 cups (720 ml) broth, garlic and a sprinkle of salt and pepper in a slow cooker. Cover and cook on low for 3 to 4 hours. Once cooked, add the remaining 1 cup (240 ml) broth and stir to combine until desired consistency is reached. Stir in the pesto, peas and lemon juice and cover, heating for about 2 to 3 minutes. Top with pecorino and serve.

BROTH-POACHED TURKEY BREAST AND LEMON THYME GRAVY

The vibrant flavor of thyme combined with the citrus flavor of lemon make for a great combination in this dish. I don't use turkey in a lot of my dishes, so this is a great one to add into your meal rotation for the week, when trying to come up with new proteins.

SERVES 4 TO 6

1 tbsp (15 ml) extra-virgin olive oil

7 tbsp (100 g) unsalted butter, divided

2 lb (900 g) turkey breast fillets, skin on

Sea salt to taste, we recommend Selina Naturally Celtic

Freshly cracked black pepper, to taste

4 shallots, peeled and cut in half

3 cups (720 ml) Chicken Bone Broth (page 10)

10 sprigs lemon thyme, plus more

1 tbsp (5 g) lemon zest, finely shredded

1 tbsp (10g) arrowroot

2 tbsp (30 ml) cold water

Heat the oil and half of the butter in a large heavy-based saucepan over medium heat. Sprinkle the turkey with salt and pepper and add to the pan skin side down. Add the shallots. Cook the turkey for 5 minutes or until golden; turn and cook for another 5 minutes or until golden. Add the broth, lemon thyme, lemon zest and pepper to taste, and bring to a simmer. Reduce the heat to low and cook covered for 30 minutes or until cooked through. Remove the turkey from the poaching liquid, cover and set aside to keep warm. Strain the broth into a bowl, discarding the solids. Place the turkey broth back into a pan and quickly whisk in the arrowroot powder and cold water. Keep whisking until all clumps are dissolved and the sauce begins to thicken. Season the gravy with salt and pepper. Ladle the gravy over the turkey breast to serve, and garnish with fresh lemon thyme.

LEMON AND MUSHROOM CHICKEN

Most of us have a mushroom chicken dish in our dinner recipe rotation, but I think you will find that using bone broth and heavy cream takes this dish to a whole new level. Many fine French restaurants use broth and cream as a staple for sauces. You may find yourself licking your plate.

SERVES 4 TO 6

6 tbsp (90 g) butter, divided

4 cups (300 g) cremini mushrooms, sliced

6 boneless, skinless chicken breasts or thighs

Sea salt, to taste we recommend Selina Naturally Celtic

Pepper, to taste

1 cup (240 ml) Chicken Bone Broth (page 10)

1 cup (240 ml) heavy whipping cream

3 tbsp (45 ml) fresh lemon juice

½ tsp white pepper

Garlic powder

Melt 3 tablespoons (45 g) butter in a large skillet over medium heat. Add the mushrooms and sauté until tender and slightly browned. Remove with a slotted spoon and set aside. Sprinkle the chicken with salt and pepper. Melt the remaining 3 tablespoons (45 g) butter in a skillet. Add the chicken and sauté 5 to 6 minutes on each side or until golden brown. Transfer the chicken to a serving platter and keep warm. Add the broth to the skillet, scraping up the browned bits. Bring to a boil, reduce the heat and simmer until reduced to approximately ¾ cup (180 ml). Stir in the cream and lemon juice. Cook over medium heat until slightly thickened. Stir in the mushrooms, white pepper, garlic powder and salt to taste. Add the chicken and simmer for 15 to 20 minutes or until the sauce is a medium-thick consistency.

SPAGHETTI SQUASH CHOW MEIN AND PRAWNS

This is a really easy dish to throw together. I use a coleslaw mix to cut down on my prep time.
You will want to use wild-caught shrimp, never farmed, as farmed can contain toxic pesticides
that upset the ecosystem and have been linked to cancer.

SERVES 4

¼ cup (60 ml) coconut aminos or gluten-free soy sauce

1 tbsp (15 g) coconut sugar

3 cloves garlic, finely chopped

1 tsp ginger, freshly grated

½ tbsp (7 ml) rice vinegar

1 tbsp (15 ml) sweet chili sauce

1 tbsp (15 ml) white wine

1 tbsp (15 ml) sesame oil

2 cloves garlic, finely chopped

⅓ small purple onion, chopped

2 green onions, diced

2 stalks celery, diced

1 lb (450 g) wild-caught shrimp, peeled, deveined

¼ cup (120 ml) Chicken Bone Broth (page 10)

1 bag coleslaw mix (about 3 to 4 cups [300 g])

1 cup (100 g) bean sprouts

1 large spaghetti squash, cooked and shredded

In a small bowl, whisk together the first seven ingredients until well mixed. Set aside.

Heat a large wok or pot over medium-high heat. Add the sesame oil. When the oil is crackling, add the garlic. Stir for 30 seconds. Add the onions and celery, and sauté until the onions soften. Once softened, add in shrimp and broth and let cook until well done, flesh is white and the broth has been absorbed, about 3 to 5 minutes. Add the coleslaw mix and bean sprouts, and stir until well mixed and the cabbage has started to wilt, another 2 to 3 minutes. Once the cabbage is soft, add the shredded spaghetti squash and sauce. Stir well and serve immediately.

THAI PEANUT CHICKEN

A client told me about this dish after her son went onto the full gut and psychology syndrome (GAPS) program. She uses it to bribe him to eat things during the week that he otherwise wouldn't touch, like sautéed liver.

SERVES 4

3 tbsp (45 ml) and 1 tsp coconut aminos or gluten-free soy sauce

2 tbsp (30 ml) and 2 tsp (10 ml) lime juice (from about 2 limes)

1 tbsp (15 ml) sesame oil, plus 1 tbsp (15 ml) more if needed

4 cloves garlic, minced

¾ tsp ground ginger

4 boneless, skinless chicken breasts or thighs

½ cup (125 g) fresh ground organic peanut butter, chunky

1 cup (240 ml) Chicken Bone Broth (page 10)

½ tsp honey

½ tsp sea salt, we recommend Selina Naturally Celtic

⅓ tsp crushed red pepper flakes

3 scallions, including green tops, chopped

In a medium, shallow glass dish or stainless steel pan, combine the 3 tablespoons (45 ml) coconut aminos, the 2 tablespoons (30 ml) lime juice, 1 tablespoon (15 ml) of the oil, the garlic and the ginger. Add the chicken and turn to coat. Let marinate for at least 10 minutes. Meanwhile, in a medium stainless steel saucepan, combine the remaining 1 teaspoon coconut aminos and 2 teaspoons (10 ml) lime juice, the peanut butter, broth, honey, salt and red pepper flakes. Pour the marinade from the chicken into the saucepan and bring just to a simmer over moderate heat, whisking until smooth. Heat a grill pan over moderate heat. Cook the chicken until browned and just done, 4 to 5 minutes per side. Remove the chicken from the pan and let it rest for 5 minutes. Cut crosswise into ¼-inch (6-mm) slices. Top the chicken with peanut sauce and chopped scallions to serve.

FENNEL ROASTED PORK BELLY

This is a recipe that has been passed around among my client base. The subtle licorice flavor in the fennel makes this pork belly sing in your mouth. Follow the dinner with sautéed apples and coconut milk whipped cream for dessert.

SERVES 4

2½ lb (1.25 kg) pork belly

Sea salt, we recommend Selina Naturally Celtic

Freshly ground black pepper

½ tbsp (2.8 g) fennel seeds

1 onion, roughly chopped

1 carrot, peeled and roughly chopped

½ stick celery, roughly chopped

½ leek, roughly chopped

2 cloves garlic, skin on, bruised

3 tbsp (2.5 g) fresh thyme

½ tsp arrowroot powder

¾ cup (180 ml) Chicken Bone Broth (page 10)

Heat the oven to 500°F (250°C). Place the pork belly onto a clean chopping board and use a sharp knife to score the skin in strips about ½ inch (1.3 cm) apart. Place the pork, belly side up, in a roasting tray and pat the skin dry using paper towels. Season the meat as well as the skin liberally with salt and pepper, and insert the fennel seeds into all the scores. Roast for about 25 to 30 minutes or until the skin has turned to crackling (golden brown and crispy). Reduce the heat to 325°F (160°C) and continue to roast the pork for 1 hour. Remove from the oven and place the onion, carrot, celery, leek, garlic and thyme under the pork. Roast for another hour or until the meat is soft and pulls apart easily. Remove from the oven and transfer the pork to a cutting board, allowing it to rest at least 15 minutes before carving. Spoon away any fat from the roasting tray and place your roasting tray directly onto the stove top. Add the arrowroot and stir, scraping up all the sediment from the bottom of the tray until a thick mushy paste is formed from all the vegetables. Stir over moderate heat for 2 minutes to cook out the raw powder. Add the broth and bring to a simmer, stirring until a gravy is formed. Season with salt and pepper to taste. Serve the pork with gravy over vegetables.

CHICKEN AND SAUSAGE GUMBO

I love serving this dish on a summer's night. Although it's a hot dish, it reminds me of our summer travels as a kid down South. Serve it with Paleo bread, and then cool off afterward with some Paleo ice cream.

SERVES 4

¼ cup (60 ml) bacon grease

3 tbsp (20 g) coconut flour

3 tbsp (20 g) almond flour

2 cups (300 g) onions, chopped

2 cups (300 g) celery, chopped

2 cups (350 g) green pepper, chopped

3 cloves garlic, minced

I qt (I L) canned tomatoes

2 cups (480 ml) Chicken Bone Broth (page 10)

2 bay leaves

½ lb (225 g) lump crabmeat, picked over for shells

½ lb (225 g) andouille sausage, sliced

I lb (450 g) wild-caught shrimp

I tbsp (5 g) gumbo (filé) powder

To make the roux, heat the bacon grease over medium-high heat and whisk in the coconut and almond flours. Stir continuously until the roux has a dark brown color (think dark peanut butter).

Add the onions, celery, peppers and garlic, and sauté until the onions are translucent and the celery is somewhat soft. Add the tomatoes, broth and bay leaves, and bring to a simmer.

Stir in the crabmeat, andouille and shrimp, and cook until the shrimp is cooked through.

Remove from the heat and stir in the gumbo powder. Serve alone or with cauliflower rice.

SEARED LAMB CHOPS
AND RED WINE REDUCTION

There is no reason to be intimidated by lamb—it's quite easy to use and it's a great protein to rotate into your food program. Remember, you can always substitute cream with coconut milk if you're a strict Paleoite.

SERVES 4

8 lamb chops, fat trimmed

Sea salt to taste, we recommend Selina Naturally Celtic

Freshly ground black pepper, to taste

½ tsp garlic powder

2 tbsp (30 ml) extra-virgin olive oil

2 garlic cloves, minced

1 large shallot, finely chopped

¾ cup (180 ml) dry red wine

1 tsp fresh rosemary, minced

1 tbsp (10 g) fresh parsley, chopped

¾ cup (180 ml) Chicken Bone Broth (page 10)

2 tsp (10 g) Dijon mustard

3 tbsp (45 ml) heavy cream

Rosemary sprigs, for garnishing

Heat a large skillet over medium-high heat. Season the lamb chops with salt, pepper and garlic powder. Add the oil to the skillet. Add the chops to the pan and cook for 4 minutes. Turn the chops over and cook 3 minutes longer until lightly browned. Remove the chops from the skillet and set aside in a warm place. Pour off all but 2 teaspoons (10 ml) of fat from skillet. Add the garlic and shallot. Cook until they become transparent and tender. Add the wine, rosemary and parsley, stirring up browned bits from the bottom of the pan. Simmer over high heat until syrupy, about 3 minutes. Add the broth and continue to simmer until the sauce is reduced by about half. Stir the mustard and cream into the sauce. Adjust seasonings. Bring to a boil, reduce to a simmer and let thicken. Remove the sauce from the heat. Place 2 chops per plate and pour sauce over the top. Garnish with a sprig of rosemary.

SHRIMP SCAMPI AND ZOODLES

Shrimp scampi is a dish that Americans love. My niece Alexandra used to gobble up this version in our restaurants when she was little. The richness of grass-fed butter, the tangy, refreshing fresh lemon and a little kick of red pepper flakes pull this dish together. Traditionally served over noodles, zoodles are our Paleo answer for this classic dish!

SERVES 4

1 tbsp (15 ml) extra-virgin olive oil

3 tbsp (45 g) butter

1 lb (450 g) wild-caught shrimp, shelled and deveined

4 cloves garlic, chopped

1 pinch crushed red pepper flakes (optional)

¼ cup (60 ml) Chicken Bone Broth (page 10)

2 tbsp (30 ml) lemon juice (about 1 lemon)

3 medium zucchini, cut into zoodles

Salt and pepper, to taste

1 tsp lemon zest

4 lemon wedges

Heat the oil and melt the butter in a pan over medium-high heat. Add the shrimp, cook for 2 minutes, flip, add the garlic and red pepper flakes and cook for 1 more minute before removing the shrimp with a slotted spoon and setting them aside. Add the broth and lemon juice to the pan to deglaze, scraping up any brown bits, and simmer for 2 minutes. Add the zucchini noodles and cook until just tender, about 2 minutes. Season with salt and pepper, and add the shrimp and lemon zest. Toss well and remove from the heat. Serve garnished with a lemon wedge.

MUSSELS IN COCONUT CURRY BROTH

Few things rival the delicious, rich and satisfying flavor of a good coconut curry broth.
Mussels are high in selenium and vitamin A, while coconut milk contains lauric acid, a beneficial
antibacterial and antiviral compound. This dish is perfect on cold winter nights!

SERVES 4

2 lb (907 g) mussels

1 tbsp (15 ml) extra-virgin olive oil

1 yellow onion, chopped

1 Thai chili, finely chopped

3 tsp (6 g) fresh ginger, minced

1½ tbsp (9 g) curry powder

½ cup (120 ml) Chicken Bone Broth
(page 10)

1 (13.5-oz [400-ml]) can coconut milk

Pinch of sea salt, we recommend Selina
Naturally Celtic

1 stalk lemongrass, chopped into four
pieces and smashed

Cilantro, chopped, for garnishing

Lime wedges

Place the mussels in a bowl of cold water to remove any sand or sediment. Let sit for 10 minutes. Drain and repeat. Remove any mussels with open shells. Debeard the mussels, pulling out their byssal threads and place them in a bowl of cold water until ready to use.

Heat the oil in a pan, add the onion and stir for a few minutes until it becomes soft and slightly translucent. Add the chili, ginger and curry powder, and stir for 1 minute until fragrant. Add the broth and reduce by half. Add the coconut milk, salt and lemongrass, and bring to a boil. Drain and add the mussels, reduce the heat to medium and cover with a tight-fitting lid. Cook for 6 to 7 minutes until the mussels open. Discard any that are closed. Spoon the mussels into bowls and pour broth over. Garnish with chopped cilantro and juice from lime wedges.

APPLE CIDER BRAISED CHICKEN

The smell of braised chicken filling your house is one that is sure to please. We love that not only is there bone broth in this recipe, but also apple cider vinegar—two superfoods! The crispy skin is a favorite, but underneath that you get tender, juicy chicken that will keep people coming back for seconds. Be sure to always use unfiltered organic apple cider vinegar.

SERVES 4

---

1 whole organic chicken, 4 to 5 lb (1.8–2.3 kg), cut up

Sea salt to taste, we recommend Selina Naturally Celtic

Freshly ground black pepper, to taste

4 slices bacon, diced

½ cup (45 g) chopped leek (white part and light green part)

½ cup (75 g) chopped onion

5 garlic cloves, peeled

1 cup (240 ml) apple cider vinegar

1 tbsp (15 g) tomato paste

4 cups (960 ml) Chicken Bone Broth (page 10)

2 or 3 sprigs fresh rosemary

1 bay leaf

Preheat the oven to 300°F (150°C). Dry the chicken well with paper towels, then season generously with salt and pepper. Cook the bacon in a heavy Dutch oven over medium-high heat until it's brown and the fat has rendered out. Add one breast, skin side down; one thigh, skin side down; one drumstick and one wing. Brown the chicken for 4 to 5 minutes, then move to a platter. Repeat with remaining pieces. Finally, brown the back, skin side down. Transfer to the platter.

To the pot, add the leeks, onion and garlic, and sauté until the onion is translucent, about 3 to 4 minutes. Pour in the vinegar, deglazing the pan and scraping off any browned bits from the bottom of the pan. Stir in the tomato paste and return all the chicken pieces to the pot. Pour in enough broth so the chicken is at least 90 percent submerged. If you need more liquid, continue adding broth. Add the rosemary and bay leaf. Bring the pot to a boil on the stovetop, cover it with a tight-fitting lid and transfer it to the oven. Cook for about 1 hour. Remove the pot from the oven. Let the chicken cool in the pot for 15 to 20 minutes before serving.

SHRIMP AND PARSNIPS IN SPICY TOMATO BROTH

For those strict Paleo followers, potatoes are one of the most missed foods. We love substituting parsnips for potatoes. Their flavor has the faint sweetness of a carrot and the texture of a potato. That sweetness pairs perfectly with this spicy tomato broth.

SERVES 4

---

2 tbsp (30 ml) extra-virgin olive oil

2 cups (300 g) finely chopped onions

4 garlic cloves, finely chopped

1 tbsp (6 g) paprika

1 (14½-oz [430-ml]) can diced fire-roasted tomatoes in juice

2 small sprigs fresh rosemary, chopped

¼ tsp crushed red pepper flakes

1 cup (240 ml) dry white wine

1 cup (240 ml) clam juice

2 cups (480 ml) Chicken Bone Broth (page 10)

1 cup (240 ml) water

8 oz (230 g) parsnips, chopped

1 lb (450 g) wild-caught shrimp, peeled and deveined

Salt and pepper, to taste

Heat the oil in a heavy large pot over medium heat. Add the onions and sauté, stirring often until very tender and beginning to brown, about 18 minutes. Add the garlic and paprika, and stir for 2 minutes. Stir in the tomatoes with juice and cook until very thick, stirring frequently, about 30 minutes. Stir in the rosemary and crushed red pepper. Add the wine and cook until the liquid evaporates completely, stirring often for about 10 minutes. Stir in the clam juice, bone broth and water, and bring to a boil. Add the parsnips and simmer until almost tender, about 5 minutes. Add the shrimp and simmer until just cooked through, about 5 minutes longer. Season with salt and pepper.

KELP NOODLE RAMEN WITH RARE BEEF

My oldest son, Clayton, could live on ramen. But he wouldn't dare touch the shelf brands.
When he was a toddler, we would take him to Chinatown in Los Angeles, and he would slurp up
the ramen bowls until he had a stomachache! This is my version of a healthy ramen bowl. Don't be afraid
of the kelp noodles. After a little rinsing in water, they are almost flavorless and you can hardly tell
the difference between real noodles and the kelp noodles.

SERVES 4

6 cups (1.5 L) Chicken Bone Broth
(page 10)

1 tsp fresh grated ginger

1 tbsp (15 ml) fish sauce

1 tsp chopped garlic

1 (14-oz [396-g]) package kelp
noodles, rinsed

4 oz (115 g) shiitake mushrooms,
cleaned and sliced

2 large organic eggs, whisked

Sea salt to taste, we recommend
Selina Naturally Celtic

Pepper, to taste

½ lb (225 g) grass-fed flank steak, thinly
sliced

1 bunch scallions, chopped

¼ cup (15 g) cilantro, chopped

1 lime, cut into wedges

Place the broth in a large saucepan over medium-high heat. Add the ginger, fish sauce, garlic and kelp noodles, and bring to a boil. Lightly boil for about 20 to 25 minutes or until the kelp noodles begin to soften. Add the mushrooms and eggs to the pot and boil for another 3 to 4 minutes. Reduce to a simmer. Add salt and pepper to taste. Gently drop steak into the hot broth and cook for 30 seconds to 1 minute or until rare. Ladle the soup into bowls and top each with scallions, cilantro and a lime wedge.

TOMATO BROTH-POACHED SEA BASS WITH ARTICHOKES

Sea bass is a great fish to introduce to children or adults who don't really care for fish. It is light and flaky. The zesty orange and strong, pungent kalamata olives pair beautifully in this dish.

SERVES 4

1 small onion, quartered and thinly sliced

2 tbsp (30 ml) extra-virgin olive oil, divided

2 garlic cloves, chopped

⅓ cup (80 ml) dry white wine

1 (9-oz [240-g]) package frozen artichoke hearts, thawed and drained

1 (15-oz [445-ml]) can stewed tomatoes

⅓ cup (60 g) pitted kalamata olives, chopped

⅔ cup (160 ml) Chicken Bone Broth (page 10)

1¼ tsp (6 g) sea salt, divided, we recommend Selina Naturally Celtic

½ tsp black pepper, divided

4 black sea bass fillets (½-inch [1.3-cm] thick) with skin

1 tbsp (15 g) unsalted butter, cut into bits

1 tsp fresh orange zest, finely grated

Preheat the oven to 325°F (160°C). Cook the onion in 2 tablespoons (30 ml) oil in a 2-quart (2-L) heavy saucepan over moderate heat, stirring occasionally until softened, about 6 minutes. Add the garlic and cook, stirring for 1 minute. Add the wine and bring to a boil and boil for about 1 minute. Add the artichoke hearts, tomatoes (including juice), olives, broth, ½ teaspoon salt and ¼ teaspoon pepper, and bring to a simmer, uncovered, stirring occasionally. Meanwhile, pat the fish dry and sprinkle with the remaining ¾ teaspoon salt and ¼ teaspoon pepper. Transfer the sauce to a glass or ceramic baking dish and arrange the fish (without crowding) over the sauce. Dot the fish with butter and cover the dish tightly with foil. Roast until the fish is just opaque and cooked through, 12 to 14 minutes. To serve, ladle the broth over the fish and serve garnished with orange zest.

BONE BROTH COQ AU VIN

I used to work as a waitress in a tiny French restaurant in Pasadena as I worked my way through college. The chef was a crazy, screaming nut case, but he cooked like an angel sent from heaven. Go figure! This is my version of his coq au vin. Bon appétit! Coq au vin is a braised wine dish. The bone broth and wine make the perfect pair for braising.

SERVES 4

2 tbsp (30 ml) extra-virgin olive oil

4 slices thick-cut bacon, sliced

1 small onion, diced

2 carrots, peeled and sliced into 1-inch (2.5-cm) pieces

1 cup (100 g) sliced mushrooms

3 small bay leaves

1 tsp dried thyme leaves

4 cloves garlic, finely minced

1 lb (450 g) boneless, skinless chicken breasts, cut into 2-inch (5-cm) chunks

1 (8-oz [235-ml]) can crushed tomatoes

1 cup (240 ml) Chicken Bone Broth (page 10)

1 cup (240 ml) red wine (cabernet or burgundy)

Salt and pepper, to taste

Mashed cauliflower, for serving

In a 4-quart (3.75-L) cast-iron saucepan, heat the olive oil over medium heat. Add the bacon, onion, carrots, mushrooms, bay leaves and thyme. Cook, stirring occasionally until very fragrant, about 5 minutes. Add the garlic, stir and cook for 1 minute. Next, add the chicken and cook for 3 to 4 minutes until seared on the outside. Stir in the tomatoes, broth and wine. Add a pinch of salt and a few grinds of black pepper. Bring the mixture to a boil, lower the heat to a simmer and let simmer for 1 hour, stirring occasionally. Serve over mashed cauliflower.

CHICKEN FAJITA LETTUCE WRAPS

I only use butter lettuce for wraps because it almost seems like that is what the leaves are made for—wrapping food! When you place the individual little lettuce leaves in your hands, they almost curl up like a taco shell. Let your children wrap their own; kids love to get creative with food and are more likely to eat it when they do.

SERVES 4 TO 6

1 cup (40 g) packed cilantro leaves, plus extra for serving

¼ cup (60 ml) lime juice, about 2 limes

¼ cup (60 ml) Chicken Bone Broth (page 10)

3 scallions, cut into 1-inch (2.5-cm) pieces

2 cloves garlic

1 jalapeño, seeded if desired

1 tbsp (15 ml) honey

Sea salt to taste, we recommend Selina Naturally Celtic

1½ lb (700 g) boneless, skinless chicken breasts

2 orange bell peppers, quartered, seeds removed

1 red onion, sliced into ½-inch (1.3-cm) thick rounds

1 ripe avocado, halved

½ cup (120 ml) water

1½ tsp (5.5 ml) extra-virgin olive oil

⅛ tsp ground cumin

⅛ tsp ground coriander

¼ cup (60 ml) grass-fed, organic, whole milk yogurt

1 head organic, butter lettuce, leaves removed and kept intact

Place the cilantro, lime juice, broth, scallions, garlic, jalapeño, honey and salt in a blender, and purée until smooth. Reserve 2 tablespoons (30 ml), and do not wash out the blender. Put the chicken breasts in a medium bowl and the peppers and onions in another. Divide the remaining cilantro purée evenly between the chicken and the peppers and onions. Toss well to coat the chicken and vegetables and let stand at room temperature for 30 minutes. Add the avocado, water and the reserved 2 tablespoons (30 ml) cilantro sauce to the blender. Purée until smooth and season with salt. Set aside.

Heat the oil in a skillet set over medium heat until hot. Add the cumin and coriander and continue to cook until fragrant, about 30 seconds to 1 minute. Pour the spices over the yogurt and set aside for the flavors to blend. Stir before serving.

Preheat a grill to medium-high heat. Grill the chicken and vegetables, turning until the vegetables are tender and the chicken is cooked completely. Let the chicken rest for 5 minutes. Slice the onions and peppers into thin strips and then slice the chicken. Divide peppers, onions, chicken and cilantro into lettuce wraps and serve with the spiced yogurt and the avocado sauce.

BRAISED PORK SHOULDER

Yes, this dish can be the star of the show for any dinner you serve, but remember that the leftovers will make amazing tacos, enchiladas or breakfast scrambles. When using broth to braise the pork shoulder, you get plenty of nutrients while adding flavor only a real broth can add to a dish.

SERVES 4

---

2 tbsp (10 g) coriander seeds, toasted

2 tbsp (10 g) cumin seeds, toasted

1 (4-lb [2-kg]) boneless pork picnic shoulder, sliced in half along the grain

Sea salt to taste, we recommend Selina Naturally Celtic

2 tbsp (30 ml) extra-virgin olive oil

1 fennel bulb, sliced

1 large onion, sliced

4 cloves garlic, smashed and finely chopped

1 (2-inch [5-cm]) piece fresh ginger, finely grated

2 cups (480 ml) dry white wine

¼ cup (60 ml) Dijon mustard

3 bay leaves

1 bundle fresh thyme

4 cups (960 ml) Chicken Bone Broth (page 10)

Using a spice grinder, grind the coriander and cumin seeds until they are a fine powder.

Preheat the oven to 375°F (190°C). Sprinkle the pork shoulder with the ground spices and salt, then tie each piece so they cook evenly. Coat a Dutch oven with oil and bring to a high heat. Brown the first pork half on all sides. Remove pork from the pan and reserve. Pour out the fat in the pan and add a few drops of new oil. Repeat with the second pork half and remove.

Lower the heat to medium, toss in the fennel and onion and season with salt. Cook the onion and fennel until they are soft and very aromatic, 7 to 8 minutes. Add the garlic and ginger and cook 2 to 3 minutes longer. Add the wine and reduce by half. Stir in the mustard and add the bay leaves and thyme. Return the pork to the Dutch oven and add the broth to the pan until it comes halfway up the side of the pork. Add salt if needed. Bring the liquid to a boil, cover and put the Dutch oven in the preheated oven. After 1 hour, turn the pork over and add more broth to the pan if the liquid level has gone down. Cover and return to the oven for 1 more hour. Turn the pork back over and return to the oven without the lid and cook 45 minutes more. The liquid should reduce. Remove the pan from the oven, remove the pork and set it aside for 15 minutes, tented with aluminum foil. Slice to serve with onions and fennel.

6-WEEK CLEARING PROGRAM

I'm always leery of practitioners who claim they have the perfect eating plan for everyone's health. I have a client who recovered from Crohn's disease using the gut and psychology syndrome (GAPS) program created by Dr. Natasha Campbell-McBride. Sometime shortly after she was free of all the symptoms of her debilitating disease, she went to a lecture where the presenter touted the benefits of raw milk. The presenter did not take into consideration that some people cannot tolerate dairy, even raw dairy. My client decided to try raw milk and her symptoms flared.

The reason I share this story is for you to understand why I always suggest an individual approach to health. I am a person who cannot tolerate grains or raw dairy regardless of how it is prepared. I keep these items out of my food program the majority of the time. Yes, I will have a slice of cheese pizza from a pizza place we love in town that ferments their crust, uses aged raw cheese and organic toppings; however, I will typically pay for that meal by the way I feel the next day. I describe it as a food hangover. Slight headache, puffy fingers (rings feel tight), bags under my eyes, a little joint ache and sluggishness. These are signs that those foods do not sit well with me so I avoid them, regardless of what another expert nutritionist may say.

If I teach you anything, please walk away with the idea that you are an individual. Dr. Campbell-McBride describes this beautifully in her book *Gut and Psychology Program* under the heading "One Man's Meat, Is Another Man's Poison." You can log onto her website at www.doctor-natasha.com/one-mans-meat-another-mans-poison.php to read the article in its entirety. To sum it up she says in her website, "Your body is an incredibly intelligent creation! As the natural foods on this planet have been designed during the same time as your body, your inner body intelligence knows their composition, and knows what foods to choose for particular needs. All we have to do is treat this intelligence with respect. Use your senses of smell, taste, desire for food and satisfaction from eating it to guide you in your decisions: when to eat, what foods to eat and in what combinations. And remember: you are unique, so what suits your neighbor may not suit you at all."

With that said, the most effective way to find out what foods affect you is to do my 6-week clearing program. The majority of my clients must do this program in order to work with me and gain better health. After 6 weeks, you will be able to listen to your body and know what may be "meat" for you and what may be "poison." I know without a doubt that raw dairy, grains and sugar are "poison" to my body because it tells me so, not because some "expert" does.

THE REAL BONE BROTH
CLEARING PROGRAM

I started using my clearing program shortly after I graduated from Dr. Natasha Campbell-McBride's GAPS course. You can read all about the digestive tract and the science behind the idea of healing your gut in Dr. Campbell-McBride's book *Gut and Psychology Syndrome*. While I love the GAPS program, I found it to be overwhelming for many of my clients. I also discovered after walking well over 500 people through the GAPS program that many of the goals that one tries to achieve with the GAPS program can oftentimes be accomplished by a simpler version that I refer to as my clearing program.

I have used this program to help clients reverse the symptoms of so many ailments I couldn't list them all, but a few are Crohn's disease, IBS, colitis, leaky gut, diverticulitis and all related gastrointestinal issues. I've also used this program to help people with joint pain, knee pain, arthritis, skin issues, chronic fatigue syndrome, many autoimmune issues, headaches and the list goes on and on and on. However, the program can also be used as a reset. I typically do my own 6-week clearing a couple times per year.

The main idea behind the program is that you clear your digestive system, your gut, of two of the most offending items, which are grains and sugar. With up to 80 percent of your immune system residing in your gut, removing these offending items allows your body to start to heal when you eat nourishing foods and real bone broth. In essence, you will simply follow a Paleo plan for 6 weeks, which excludes grains, beans, sugar and all dairy.

My goal is to keep the clearing program really simple and to give you many choices. So let's get into the "meat" (no pun intended) of the clearing program.

THE CLEARING PROGRAM

TOSS

Clear out your pantry and throw away items such as the following:

- All denatured oils such as canola oil, vegetable oil, corn oil and cooking oil. These denatured fats cause inflammation in the body. They are also hidden culprits when eating out. You can order the most healthful dish of filet mignon with a side of vegetables, but if they use these types of oil in the restaurant, you will find yourself bloated the next day from the oil and the salt they use.

- Table salt.

- Spices that contain denatured salt such as garlic salt and onion salt, and all seasoning spices or herb blends that are not organic. These can be hidden causes of inflammation.

- All bread, cereals, grains (this includes rice, quinoa and spelt). No grains can be eaten for 6 weeks.

- Sugar and agave syrup.

Throw out your toxic household cleaning supplies, laundry and dishwashing detergent and all hygienic products, and don't use perfume or cologne ever.

From this day forward, commit to using only acceptable fats and oils such as coconut oil, palm oil, olive oil, avocado oil, ghee, butter (if tolerated), lard and duck fat.

HERBS AND SPICES

Use Celtic sea salt. My favorite brand is Selina Naturally. I love this salt because it's mined using the old-world method of air drying rather than heating in a factory. Celtic sea salt has over 80 naturally occurring minerals in it. Don't be fooled by the politically correct diet pushers who claim that salt is bad for you. Table salt is bad for you. Celtic sea salt is wonderful for your body and can lead to better health. Use it generously! Also, don't buy cheap Celtic sea salt. It is expensive to mine and keep in its natural state, so expect to pay the higher price for the good stuff!

Use only raw honey, grade B maple syrup and coconut sugar, and never use these daily.

All spices and herbs should be organic and should not have any salt added. Also, only use organic products on your body, and replace perfume and cologne with essential oils.

BE PREPARED

One way to set yourself up for failure and fall off this program is to be hungry and not have a meal or snack plan at the ready. You need to plan at least one day ahead and know what your meals and snacks will consist of. Do not fly by the seat of your pants when approaching your food program. Have a variety of snacks to choose from, and always have a quick go-to food such as frozen meatballs and marinara sauce, frozen soups or stews handy.

EAT

Most people are addicted to diets. I ban the word *diet* in my nutrition practice and replace it with the words *food program*. Diet connotes starvation. A food program implies nourishment. Remember, friends, food is medicine, and if you want the body to heal, you have to eat. With that said, you must eat while on this food-clearing program. I have had clients who did not heed this advice, and they did not get the results they needed because they were dieting. I cannot emphasize this enough (picture me shouting this at you from the rooftop), YOU MUST EAT on this food-clearing program. Here is the key: You must eat every 3 hours minimum. Now, this does not mean you pig out; you simply eat small meals or small portions every 2½ to 3 hours. This will help maintain your blood sugar levels and will help your adrenal glands stay strong throughout the process.

JOURNALING

Start a journal for your food program. List all the current symptoms you currently have, such as joint pain, constipation, headaches, acne or IBS. Record what you eat daily so if your symptoms come back, you can trace them to a particular food that may be causing them.

RECIPES

While on the clearing program, you will need to modify all of the recipes you use to ensure you eliminate dairy, grains, beans and sugar. Always eat within 45 minutes of waking up. Also, please know that I do not give recipes for every item my clients will be eating for a 6-week program. I tell my clients that they have to be active participants in gathering Paleo-friendly recipes, cooking and finding foods that appeal to them on the Internet. For instance, you if you see zucchini cakes as a snack, search the Internet for a Paleo version that appeals to you, and use that recipe. I have found this active approach sets my clients up for a lifetime of wellness, rather than simply a 6-week robotic program that doesn't teach them how to find recipes and foods that appeal to them and their preferences.

DAY 1

Eat chicken bone broth soup all day long.

BONE BROTH CHICKEN SOUP

1 whole chicken

Water, enough to cover the chicken

Chicken feet

Onion

Garlic

Sea salt, we recommend Selina Naturally Celtic

Peppercorns

Bay leaf

Carrots

Zucchini

Mushrooms

Celery

Organic herbs

Place 1 whole chicken in a large 8 to 10 quart (8–10 L) stock pot with filtered water to cover the chicken. Add chicken feet, onion, garlic, Celtic sea salt, peppercorns and bay leaf. Cook for 3 hours or until the meat is cooked. Remove the meat from the carcass, place the carcass back into the stockpot and cook for 20 hours on a very, very low simmer adding water if necessary. During the last 2 hours, add in a variety of vegetables such as carrots, zucchini, mushrooms and celery. You can include any vegetable you would like with the exception of potatoes, yams and sweet potatoes. Flavor with organic herbs of your choice.

Yep, that's it. You will eat this chicken soup (which contains the broth, the meat and the vegetables), all day long.

Here is what your day might look like:

- 7:00 a.m.: 1 big bowl of chicken soup
- 8:00 a.m.: 1 tall glass of filtered water (you will drink enough water in between your meals to equal your weight divided in half in ounces. For example, if you weigh 150 pounds [68 kg], you drink 75 ounces [2.1-L ml] of water in a day).
- 9:30 a.m.: 1 big bowl of chicken soup
- 12:00 p.m.: 1 big bowl of chicken soup
- 2:30 p.m.: 1 big bowl of chicken soup
- Do the same at 5:00 p.m., 7:30 p.m. and 9:00 p.m., before bedtime.

Okay so you get the picture here. Do not skip a serving. Eat as much as you would like. The food is the medicine, and you should not be hungry. You will find yourself eating a lot of servings of soup these first couple of days.

Note: If you are a coffee drinker, it is ideal to stop drinking coffee for the first week; however, if you tend to get migraines or headaches when you don't drink coffee or if you have no intention of giving up coffee, then you can have it with the clearing program but only after your first serving of soup. Also, do not add anything to your coffee during the first week. During the second week, you can add homemade nut milks or pure, 100 percent, coconut milk without any additives.

DAY 2

Your food program is the same as it was on Day 1. Please note that you may not feel well on this day, as though your body is coming down with a cold or flu. This is common as your body clears. The key to feeling better is to eat as much as you can. If you feel nauseous or throw up, add a pinch of sea salt (we recommend Selina Naturally Celtic) to your water a couple times throughout the day. Continue to eat all day long. I find that by the night of Day 2, most of my clients are gagging down the chicken soup! I know this doesn't sound appealing, but hang in there. On Day 3 you will be in heaven with the foods you get to start eating. Eat, eat, eat, even if you don't feel like it.

DAY 3

- BREAKFAST: Scrambled eggs sautéed in any approved fat with plenty of Celtic sea salt
- SNACK (2½ HOURS AFTER BREAKFAST): 1 large bowl of chicken soup
- LUNCH: Breakfast Mush (see page 33)
- SNACK: Mush with 1 cup (240 ml) of bone broth
- DINNER: Beef Stew

DAY 4

- BREAKFAST: 1 egg scrambled with a variety of vegetables of your choice
- SNACK: Breakfast Mush (see recipe on page 33) or chicken soup
- LUNCH: Leftover beef stew from the previous night's dinner
- SNACK: Zucchini chips (broil sliced zucchini tossed in olive oil and Celtic sea salt in the oven for 5 to 7 minutes or until almost blackened) and 1 cup (240 ml) of bone broth
- DINNER: Beef Bolognese with zucchini noodles (see recipe on page 107)

DAY 5

- BREAKFAST: Chicken soup (you should get used to having soups and stews loaded with vegetables a few days a week for breakfast. Freeze big batches so you can grab one in the morning and heat.)
- SNACK: Homemade beef jerky. Make big batches and use throughout the week. There are a variety of recipes online.

- LUNCH: Salad with a variety of vegetables, topped with apple cider vinegar, olive oil and Celtic sea salt. Small serving of leftover Beef Bolognese from the night before.
- SNACK: Zucchini or Kale chips and 1 to 2 cups (240 to 480 ml) of bone broth
- Dinner: Seared Halibut in Chorizo (see recipe on page 130)

DAY 6

- BREAKFAST: Grain-Free Savory Oatmeal (see recipe on page 117) with a side of bacon
- SNACK: Zucchini Cakes
- LUNCH: Leftover Seared Halibut from the previous night
- DINNER: Loaded vegetable salad with grilled chicken

DAY 7

- BREAKFAST: Bacon and Tomato Breakfast Casserole (see recipe on page 18)
- SNACK: Chicken soup
- LUNCH: Another serving of breakfast casserole or salad loaded with veggies, fish and 1 cup (240 ml) of bone broth
- SNACK: Beef jerky and zucchini chips
- DINNER: Coconut Curry and Lime Soup (see recipe on page 97)

At this point you should have completed 7 days of my clearing program. You may find that you have lost 5 to 10 pounds (2.2 to 4.5 kg), or you may have maintained your weight if you didn't need to lose any. Many of the complaints you recorded in your journal have disappeared or lessened. Your body is clearing itself of toxins, and you should start to have more energy.

You will model day 7, above, for the next 5 weeks. Here is an example of what your day may look like from this point forward:

- BREAKFAST IDEAS: An egg scramble sautéed in coconut oil with a variety of vegetables added, soups, stews, egg casseroles, bacon lettuce wraps with tomatoes and avocado, breakfast mush, sausages rolled up in coconut flour pancakes.
- SNACK IDEAS: Homemade beef jerky, kale or zucchini chips, Paleo zucchini cakes, sausages rolled up in coconut flour pancakes, hard-boiled eggs, small salads, small servings of soup.
- LUNCH AND DINNER IDEAS: A variety of proteins and vegetables that you rotate daily.

Here are key points to ensuring your success in the program:

- Drink the amount of water I suggested for you daily.

- Try not to eat out at restaurants because of the hidden oils and bad salt in restaurant food.

- Rotate your proteins and your vegetables daily.

- Do not get into food ruts by eating the same thing every day. This is not a healthy way of eating. You need to rotate vegetables and colors of vegetables daily. The same goes for proteins.

- Allow yourself one dinner a week with vegetables only, no protein.

- Refrain from consuming beer, wine and alcohol during the 6-week program.

- Do not eat fruit for the first 6 weeks.

- No grains or sugar at all, this includes rice and quinoa.

If you feel sluggish, bloated, tired or as though you have a slight hangover when you wake up in the morning, it is most likely because you ate something that your body is sensitive to. Remove that item and keep it out of your food program for the rest of the 6-week period. After 6 weeks, reintroduce that food item. If you still can't tolerate it, you most likely don't do well with that particular food so you shouldn't eat it. For example, I don't do well with nuts or grains. No matter how I soak them, dehydrate them, massage them, etc., I can't digest them well so I don't eat them.

The cleaner your body is, the more in tune you will be with what foods your body prefers. Watch for signs and add and remove foods accordingly. Your body is telling you what it likes and what it doesn't like.

After you've completed the 6 weeks of the clearing program, you can start to add foods like raw dairy, rice and fruit back into your diet. You will know if these foods agree with you by the way you feel and the symptoms you are experiencing.

Keep drinking bone broth, and use it as a base for cooking your foods. The broth helps keep the mucosal lining sealed and your immune system strong.

RESOURCES
SOME OF OUR FAVORITE THINGS

WEBSITES

www.RealBoneBroth.com

RealTrueFoods.com

www.GAPS.me to find a GAPS practitioner in your area

BOOKS

Davis, William. *Wheat Belly: Lose the Wheat, Lose the Weight, and Find Your Path Back to Health*. Emmaus, Penn.: Rodale, 2011.

Fallon, Sally, and Mary G. Enig. *Nourishing Traditions: The Cookbook that Challenges Politically Correct Nutrition and the Diet Dictocrats*. Rev. 2nd ed. Brandywine, MD: NewTrends Pub., 2001.

Genzlinger, Kelly, and Kathy Erlich. *Super Nutrition for Babies: The Right Way to Feed Your Baby for Optimal Health*. Beverly, MA: Fair Winds Press, 2012.

Graham, Gray, and Deborah Kesten. *Pottenger's Prophecy: How Food Resets Genes for Wellness or Illness*. Amherst, Mass.: White River Press, 2010.

Henderson, Bill. *Cancer-Free: Your Guide to Gentle, Non-Toxic Healing*. 2nd ed. Bangor, ME: Booklocker.com, 2007.

McBride, Natasha. *Gut and Psychology Syndrome: Natural Treatment for Autism, Dyspraxia, A.D.D., Dyslexia, A.D.H.D., Depression, Schizophrenia*. Rev. and Expanded ed. Cambridge, U.K.: Medinform Pub, 2010.

Newport, Mary T. *Alzheimer's Disease, What If There Was a Cure?: The Story of Ketones*. Laguna Beach, CA: Basic Health Publications, 2011.

Perlmutter, David, and Kristin Loberg. *Grain Brain: The Surprising Truth about Wheat, Carbs, and Sugar—your Brain's Silent Killers*. Boston: Little Brown & Co., 2013.

Shanahan, Catherine, and Luke Shanahan. *Deep Nutrition: Why Your Genes Need Traditional Food*. Lawai, HI: Big Box Books, 2009.

Sisson, Mark. *The Primal Blueprint*. London: Vermilion, 2012.

Tam, Michelle, and Henry Fong. *Nom Nom Paleo: Food for Humans*. Kansas City, Missouri: Andrews McMeel Publishing, 2013.

Walker, Danielle. *Against All Grain: Delectable Paleo Recipes to Eat Well & Feel Great: More than 150 Gluten-Free, Grain-Free, and Dairy-Free Recipes for Daily Life*. Las Vegas: Victory Belt Pub., 2013.

ACKNOWLEDGMENTS

It is a rare moment when a mom can be thankful for her child's illness. However, I am thankful that my son Blake experienced chronic health issues as a baby and small child. Blake would agree that he would go through all of it again, as it was his sickness that made me pursue alternative care and allowed me to help so many people regain their health in my nutrition practice and through our product Real Bone Broth. So Blakey, thanks for being the bridge to real, true health! And thanks to my other two children, Clayton and Camden, for eating good food and taking handfuls of supplements daily.

There are many more people I would like to thank:

My husband, Reb, whom I met in 1989 when he was a chef in an amazing restaurant in Pasadena, California, where we started our love affair for one another and all things related to good food. It's been a ride, Mr. Wonderful.

My niece Alexandra Rains, who helped pour out her heart and knowledge of cooking and wellness into these recipes. How can a 27-year-old know so much about good food? She really deserves to have her name on the front cover of this book. Her passion for good food began when as a little girl she would sit at our restaurants and watch the chefs do their magic. Thanks for the late nights and recipe madness.

Dr. Cate Shanahan, the author of *Deep Nutrition*, who shows us a practical scientific approach to food, health and wellness. I love her book and tell all of my clients it is a must-read. Dr. Cate has influenced my approach to food, nutrition and wellness not only for my family, but for my clients as well.

Mark Sisson, of Mark's Daily Apple, the Father of Paleo, for taking the Paleo approach mainstream and giving all of us such great information on his website and in his book *The Primal Blueprint*. His primal mayonnaise is to die for.

Michelle Tam, blogger extraordinaire, cookbook author of *Nom Nom Paleo: Food for Humans*. Michelle, you are quite possibly one of the nicest people Reb and I have met.

The thousands of clients of mine who have taken my nutrition advice and have recovered from illnesses that seemed otherwise irreversible. Thanks for believing that food could be your medicine and for doing the hard work.

Dr. Weston A. Price for pioneering the pursuit of nutrition and its effect on teeth.

Simon Gorman from Wise Choice Market. Thanks for believing in our broth and providing an avenue for people all over the United States to purchase our Real Bone Broth.

Kim Schuette, of Biodynamic Wellness, who first introduced me to the cookbook *Nourishing Traditions*. It is this very book that taught me the benefits of bone broth and how to make it for my son Blake.

Gray Graham and the Nutritional Therapy Association for teaching nutritionists around the world the proper approach to wellness.

ABOUT THE AUTHORS

SHARON BROWN is a clinical nutritionist, nutritional therapist and a certified GAPS practitioner. She has a thriving private nutrition practice in Del Mar, California, and is the creator of the brand Real Bone Broth.

Her interest in alternative health care became personal when her second son was born in 1999. Her son suffered from chronic ear infections, sinus infections and rashes. After following the conventional medical approach and what she refers to as the "antibiotic train" for six years, she decided there had to be a better way. She started to follow a whole food nutritional approach for her son, allowing food to be his medicine. Gone were all of the boxed and pantry foods, which were replaced by real food and lots of bone broth. Within 6 months, her son was free of his chronic issues, and he has never had another ear infection, sinus infection or rash. This led Sharon to go back to school to study nutrition so she could share in a professional setting what she had learned.

Sharon has worked with thousands of clients across the nation, using bone broth as a staple to healing chronic ailments and as an addition to any wellness program. She found her clients to be reluctant to make their own bone broth and could not find a real bone broth brand on the market. This led her and her professionally trained chef husband, Reb, to make their own brand, called Real Bone Broth. Today their broth is the fastest-growing bone broth brand on the market and can be found in stores and online all over the country. Incorporating bone broth into every recipe is the key to her clients' success in their wellness journeys. This cookbook is a compilation of recipes that she and her husband created, as well as recipes from her clients who have used broth to heal and stay healthy.

INDEX